RESEARCH METHODS IN SOCIAL RELATIONS

RESEARCH
METHODS

IN SOCIAL RELATIONS

Third Edition

CLAIRE SELLTIZ
Department of Psychology, City University of New York

LAWRENCE S. WRIGHTSMAN
Department of Psychology, University of Kansas

STUART W. COOK
Department of Psychology, University of Colorado

In Collaboration with
GEORGE I. BALCH
Department of Political Science
University of Illinois, Chicago Circle
RICHARD HOFSTETTER
Department of Political Science, Ohio State University
LEONARD BICKMAN
Department of Psychology, Loyola University of Chicago

HOLT, RINEHART AND WINSTON
New York   Chicago   San Francisco   Atlanta   Dallas   Montreal   Toronto

Library of Congress Cataloging in Publication Data

Main entry under title:

Research methods in social relations.

"Published for the Society for the Psychological
Study of Social Issues (SPSSI)"
    Bibliography: p. 583
    Includes indexes.
    1. Social science research. I. Selltiz, Claire.
II. Society for the Psychological Study of Social Issues.
H62.R45   1976   300'.7'2   76-2004
ISBN: 0-03-080986-X (College Edition)
ISBN: 0-03-910271-8 (International Edition)

Grateful acknowledgment is made to the following for the use of copyrighted materials:

Academic Press for text from R. Christie and F. L. Geis, *Studies in Machiavellianism*, 1970.

Addison-Wesley Publishing Company, Inc., for text from George J. McCall, The problem of indicators in participant observation research, in George J. McCall and J. L. Simmons, *Issues in participant observation: A text and reader*, 1969, Addison-Wesley, Reading, Mass.

American Sociological Association for data from H. Carter, Recent American studies in attitudes toward war: A summary and evaluation, *American Sociological Review*, 1945, *10*, 343–352. From K. Marquis, Effects of social reinforcement on health reporting in the household interview, *Sociometry*, 1970, *33*, 203–215.

The Center for Political Studies of the Institute for Social Research at the University of Michigan for text adapted from The 1972 Pre-Election Study, Section E, Form II.

B. G. Glaser for text from The constant comparative method of quantitative analysis, *Social Problems*, 1965, *12*, 436–445. © 1965 by the Society for the Study of Social Problems.

Holt, Rinehart and Winston for text from *Studying behavior in natural settings*, by R. M. Brandt. Copyright © 1972 by Holt, Rinehart and Winston, Inc. From *Personality and interpersonal behavior*, by R. F. Bales. Copyright © 1970 by Holt, Rinehart and Winston, Inc.

Law and Society Association for tables from D. T. Campbell and H. L. Ross, The Connecticut crackdown on speeding: Time-series data in quasi-experimental analysis, *Law and Society Review*, 1968, *3*(1), 33–76. *Law and Society Review* is the official publication of the Law and Society Association.

Leo Lowenthal and Pacific Books for table from *Literature, popular culture, and society*, 1961. Pacific Books, Publishers, Palo Alto, Calif.

Oxford University Press for text from *Race attitudes in South Africa*, by I. D. MacCrone, 1937.

To Caroline Weichlein, whose impact is felt on every page
—in many more ways than just one.

PREFACE

A cursory reading of the front page of today's newspaper indicates to all of us the enormity of social problems in our contemporary world. Today's headlines may deal with Arab–Israeli hostilities, or with protests against crosstown busing for school desegregation, or with the unemployment rate in the inner city. Whatever they say, they demand solutions—as rapidly as possible.

Solutions must be based on knowledge, and the act of acquiring and evaluating knowledge is a continuous one. The purpose of this book is to bring together at an introductory level the considerations that enter into every step of the knowledge-gathering process as it relates to social phenomena. The book is appropriate for use in undergraduate courses on research methods in a number of departments, including political science, social work, sociology, psychology, and social psychology.

Research methods may be presented in many different ways. The special emphasis of our presentation arises from a continuing concern among social scientists that their work should contribute to the solution of practical problems as they arise in the contemporary world. Experience has demonstrated that research conducted without concern for immediate application is neither easily nor promptly put to use. Research concerned with immediate application requires, throughout the research process, a collaborative effort between social scientists and those who act upon their findings. Such collaboration creates problems of its own, for which neither set of partners is fully prepared by their specific training or experience. We believe that this book will aid in bridging the gap.

While the knowledge-gathering process goes on, its concepts and methods may change. This third edition reflects new developments and concerns. For example, Chapter 13, Data Processing, is a new chapter dealing with coding and data reduction, the steps in preparing data for machine processing, the use of computer programs, and the accumulated wisdom about the use of computers.

Chapter 7, also new, reflects the highly important questions about the ethics of social research. This chapter, written by the chairperson of the committee that revised the American Psychological Association's ethics code, describes a number of ethically questionable practices in social research, and presents a cost-benefits analysis for evaluating individual research proposals.

Another major addition is Chapter 2, The Logic of Analysis, which considers the philosophy of science underlying the social research process. A much updated chapter on observational methods (Chapter 8) describes new developments using this approach.

All chapters have been updated and have been extensively revised where needed. The main emphasis of the book is now on the use of multiple methods to eliminate alternative hypotheses and to overcome the limitations inherent in any single method. Moreover, this revision emphasizes the intellectual unity of research and serious thought; research methods are an extension of the latter, rather than simply a bag of gimmicks and gadgets. The inclusion of an entire chapter on the ethical questions of research (Chapter 7) reflects this theme of the intellectual status of research as a knowledge-generating activity. Also, as a study aid for the student, we have included a glossary of important terms at the end of the text. In addition, these terms appear in the margin of the text pages where they are discussed.

From the initiation of the planning for the first edition more than twenty-five years ago, this book has been sponsored by the Society for the Psychological Study of Social Issues (SPSSI). An organization composed of social scientists and other persons with similar interests, SPSSI's goal is to facilitate the application of social science knowledge to the solution of society's problems. Throughout its three editions, the officers and Council of SPSSI have supported this book by providing editorial guidance and financial support. The production of the first edition might not have been possible without the prompt and generous financial assistance of the Anti-Defamation League of B'nai B'rith, the National Conference of Christians and Jews, and the United Nations Educational, Scientific and Cultural Organization.

We are also indebted to a number of colleagues for their generous contributions of time and thought to this revision. Harold Proshansky of the City University of New York and Richard Schmuck of the University of Oregon served as Publications Chairpersons of SPSSI during the planning and initial preparation of this edition. Two recent Presidents of SPSSI, Albert Pepitone of the University of Pennsylvania and Harry C. Triandis of the University of

Illinois at Champaign-Urbana, provided the momentum for the completion of the revision.

The initial drafts of the chapters were done by a number of social scientists from several disciplines. George I. Balch of the Department of Political Science at the University of Illinois, Chicago Circle, and Richard Hofstetter of the Department of Political Science at Ohio State University drafted major portions of Chapters 1, 2, 5, 6, 9, 10, 12, and 13. John Kirscht of the School of Public Health at the University of Michigan reorganized and updated an early draft of Chapter 5. The initial revision of Chapter 4 was prepared by Louise Kidder of the Department of Psychology at Temple University. Leonard Bickman of the Department of Psychology at Loyola University of Chicago wrote Chapter 8 on observational methods. Isidor Chein of the Department of Psychology at New York University prepared Appendix A on sampling.

For individual chapters, a number of social scientists aided us by reacting to chapter drafts or by suggesting needs for revision. These include David C. Leege, Department of Political Science, University of Illinois, Chicago Circle, for Chapter 2; Donald W. Fiske, Committee for Behavioral Science, University of Chicago, for Chapters 2, 6, and 9; Barbara Dohrenwend, Department of Psychology, City University of New York, for Chapters 4, 9, and 12; Homer Johnson, Department of Psychology, Loyola University of Chicago, for Chapters 6 and 11; Howard Sandler, Faculty in Psychology, George Peabody College for Teachers, for Chapter 6; Ellen Berscheid, Department of Psychology, University of Minnesota, for Chapter 7; Morton Deutsch, Department of Psychology, Teachers College, Columbia University, for Chapter 7; Charles F. Cannell, Survey Research Center, University of Michigan, for Chapter 9; Thomas Ostrom, Department of Psychology, Ohio State University, for Chapter 12; and James Wiley, Department of Sociology, University of Illinois, Chicago Circle, for Chapter 14. Within the limits of our time and resources, we have tried to follow the suggestions offered by these colleagues. However, they should not be held responsible for our sins of omission or commission.

The manuscript of this revision was also examined by a SPSSI ad hoc committee concerned with the effects of sexism, racism, and classism in research design, interpretation of data, and in the language used in the text. This committee was composed of Jeanne Block, Wendell Rivers, Joe Trimble, and Judy Rosenblith (Chairperson). In line with their concerns, we have sought in this revision to identify and disparage ways that social science research has been used to discriminate against certain groups in our society. For example, social science research has been used to justify existing social values; there has been discrimination against certain groups when the subjects of the study are selected; and unfair comparisons between groups are often made. At several points throughout this book, we discuss these biases in more detail. In doing so, we have also responded to the detailed and useful comments of Suzanne Prescott and Alice Dan of Women in Research.

Additionally, we have tried to eliminate the use of sexist language in this revision.

A number of instructors in research methods courses also examined a draft of the manuscript. They include Kirk W. Elifson of the Department of Sociology, Georgia State University; Audrey Olsen Faulkner of the Graduate School of Social Work, Rutgers University; and Michael Phillips of the School of Social Work, Hunter College.

The act of transforming scribbles on yellow tablets into a finished book is a complex one. Caroline Weichlein and Barbara Kelly of the SPSSI central office staff performed magnificently in typing and retyping drafts, proofreading them, tracking down references, obtaining permissions, and otherwise handling the myriad of details connected with the completion of a book manuscript. In all cases they acted with patience and speed. Shirley Wrightsman prepared the index under great time pressures. Doreen Lovelace typed portions of the material and handled correspondence associated with the production of the book.

The staff of Holt, Rinehart and Winston, especially Deborah Doty and Johnna Barto, have been most helpful in the task of seeing this project through to publication. We wish there were a better way to acknowledge the contributions of all these people; perhaps it is enough to say to them: Here is the book—it is as much yours as it is the authors!

February 1976
Claire Selltiz
Lawrence S. Wrightsman
Stuart W. Cook

CONTENTS

appendix **B**
QUESTIONNAIRE CONSTRUCTION AND INTERVIEW PROCEDURE
Arthur Kornhauser and *Paul B. Sheatsley*   541

chapter 1

WHY DO RESEARCH?

I. THE FUNCTIONS OF RESEARCH

To research is to search again, to take another, more careful look, to find out more. We take another look because something may be wrong with what we already know. Is research necessary? Isn't plain old common sense enough? At times it is. But that it *may* be enough is no guarantee that it *must* be. We must recognize that it is possible to be right for the wrong reasons. For instance, it used to be common sense that the world is relatively flat; anyone could see that by *just looking*. But "just looking" does not always yield valid conclusions.

What the research attitude presumes is that the first look—and every later look—may be prone to error, so that one must look again and again, differently and thoroughly each time. Each method of investigation may have its own particular limits. We must try to make ourselves aware of these limits so that we can transcend them or at least not be taken in by them. As the nineteenth-century American humorist Artemus Ward once said, "It ain't the things we don't know that get us in trouble. It's the things we know that ain't so."

Let us return to just looking as a method of knowing. What is involved in that method? Christopher Columbus and King Ferdinand are standing on the west coast of Spain, staring at the Atlantic Ocean. A Spanish ship has just set sail for parts unknown, and the two men watch it disappear below the horizon. Columbus believed the world was round, and Ferdinand believed it was relatively flat—or at least hump-backed, like a turtle. Do the two men see the same thing? Columbus sees the ship taking its first curve around the world, while Ferdinand only sees it disappearing from view. Or take another example: "Would an infant see what you see here when you see words and sentences and he sees but marks and lines?" (Hanson, 1958, p. 16).

As Hanson said, "there is more to seeing than meets the eyeball" (1958, p. 7). When we look, what we see differs according to what we know,

2

think, or expect. So, even just looking involves previous training, experience, or knowledge. But we are often unaware of that, and so we attribute our observations entirely to the object being observed, rather than to some combination of the object and the observer (ourselves). And because we are unaware of our biases, we do not question them. Just looking is smug ignorance.

Discussions of research methods usually include some lengthy, persuasive paragraphs about the importance of theory for research. But all observation uses some theory. All investigation must make use of some categories, since it is impossible (and undesirable) to notice everything at once. The language we use to think about objects does much of the selection for us. For instance, the Arabic language contains more than seven hundred words related to the camel. Why so many? Because some Arabs need to *notice* these things about the camel in order to survive in the desert. Such assumptions about the world are built into our very language and our concepts. That is why no special section is needed here on theory and research, for research *must* make assumptions as it tests theories about the world. How else could it be?

Earlier we implied that common sense is a perception-screening device. But so is research. Where the two differ most critically is that research systematically makes explicit and challengeable its bases for screening and challenges them as a matter of course. Research does this in two ways: by testing the old screens and by creating new, alternative ones.

Let us take some examples of what appear to be factual statements along with the commonsensical rationale for each:

1. When a number of people witness an emergency, they are more likely to help the victim than if only one person is a witness. (There is "safety in numbers.") (Latané and Darley, 1970)
2. Blacks participate less in politics than do whites. (The effects of poverty have discouraged Blacks from political action.) (Cataldo, Johnson, and Kellstedt, 1968)
3. The most frequent disapproval of United States entry into the Vietnam war between 1965 and 1969 came from American youth. (Everyone knows that young people are more rebellious and curious than older people. Besides, look at the demonstrators.) (Rosenberg, Verba, and Converse, 1970)
4. In the New Hampshire Democratic presidential primary election of 1968, those who voted for Senator Eugene McCarthy were demonstrating their dovish position on the Vietnam war. (McCarthy's only platform at the time was peace.) (Converse, Miller, Rusk, and Wolfe, 1969)
5. The most poorly educated, the poorest, the unemployed, and recent emigrants from the South were more likely than other Blacks to participate in the ghetto riots of the 1960s. (Such "riffraff" have not learned the norms of civil society.) (Fogelson and Hill, 1968)

These statements might seem to be so obvious that it would become embarrassingly wasteful to research them. Yet, they have all been researched. *And they have all been disconfirmed, at least in some situations.* When several witnesses hear a person call out in trouble, they expect one of the other witnesses to help, while a solitary observer knows it is up to him to respond; Blacks in Buffalo, New York, participate as much as whites in most kinds of political activities and *more* frequently than whites in some kinds, despite their greater poverty; the *least* frequent disapproval of the United States involvement in the Vietnam war has come regularly from American youth; and so on. (The references after each statement above give the source of the actual findings.)

A list like this was presented back in 1949 by Paul Lazarsfeld to discuss the findings of a major study titled *The American Soldier.* As Lazarsfeld has pointed out:

> If we had mentioned the actual results of the investigation first, the reader would have labelled these "obvious" also. Obviously, something is wrong with the entire argument of "obviousness." It should really be turned on its head. Since every kind of human reaction is conceivable, it is of great importance to know which reactions actually occur most frequently and under what conditions; only then will a more advanced social science develop (1969, p. 380).

Common sense limits people to the familiar. For instance, you were probably surprised to learn that youth were the age group most supportive of the Vietnam war, because most of your friends did not support it, and because the student antiwar demonstrations of the 1960s were highly publicized. But most youth of the 1960s were not in college, most college students were not in liberal arts and sciences, most colleges had no demonstrations, and most liberal arts and science students were not involved in the demonstrations that did occur. In short, you are familiar with an unrepresentative minority. The same kind of limited perception occurred among supporters of Senator Goldwater's presidential bid in 1964 and Senator McGovern's in 1972, achieving their party's nomination but ending in resounding defeat (Converse, Miller, and Clausen, 1965).

While every kind of human reaction is conceivable, not everyone can conceive of every kind of reaction. For instance, consider this riddle: A man and his son are in an automobile accident. The man is killed and the boy, seriously injured, is rushed to the hospital for surgery. But the surgeon takes one look at him and says, "I'm sorry, but I can't operate on this boy. He is my son." According to the riddle, the boy's father is dead and the surgeon is telling the truth. How can that be?

Many North Americans find this riddle insoluble. Yet, the answer is simple: The surgeon is the boy's mother. This answer never occurs to some people. They are not accustomed to thinking that a surgeon might be a woman. In the United States (but not everywhere) the surgeons are almost always men. People may come to regard the familiar as inevitable and the unfamiliar as inconceivable.

When a person's sources of information—parents, friends, religion, teachers, and the mass media—are all in agreement, his or her ideas may be limited to a nonconscious ideology,

> . . . a set of beliefs and attitudes which he accepts implicitly but which remains outside his awareness because alternative conceptions of the world remain unimagined. . . . [O]nly a very unparochial and intellectual fish is aware that his environment is wet. After all, what else could it be? Such is the nature of a nonconscious ideology (Bem, 1970, p. 89).

Science, by *taking as problematic* nonconscious ideologies, can go beyond their parochial cultural bounds. To do scientific research, one might say, is to challenge accepted beliefs by submitting them to scrutiny through the use of demanding standards.

By contrast, as Nagel (1961) said: "[C]ommon-sense beliefs are not subjected, as a matter of established principle, to systematic scrutiny in the light of data secured for the sake of determining the accuracy of those beliefs and the range of their validity" (p. 12). Scientists are professional troublemakers: they must challenge old beliefs, create new ones, and then turn the challenge upon those new ones.

Social science research not only corrects perception; it expands it. In contrast, because of its exclusive concern with immediate specific application rather than explanation through general principles, common sense cannot readily deal with new problems. When social change occurs, the old prediction rules may not work. But if we know why they worked in the first place, we also know why they no longer work. Or, rules which work in one social setting will not work in another. In a time of rapid social change and increasing permeability of institutions, general explanations are wanted more than ever. Thus, by generating new concepts and explanations, social science can heighten our awareness of where things fit in a larger framework.

Similarly, common-sense concern with the immediate often results in coexisting contradictory beliefs. For instance, we have been told that "opposites attract." We also know that "birds of a feather flock together." To take another example, some politicians believe that the way for them to lose an election is to increase governmental expenditures, while others believe that such expenditures can provide jobs and help their reelection. In both examples, there are cases that support each of the contradictory beliefs. However, in a study of gubernatorial elections from 1948 to 1964, Gerald Pomper (1968) found both political beliefs to be *generally incorrect*. The general trend in voting for one of the parties counts much more toward the election outcome than does variation in government spending and taxing. "Marginal differences from these trends, however, can be gained by policies which broaden a state executive's coalition beyond that normally associated with the party" (Pomper, 1968, p. 139). In other words, a Republican who spends and a Democrat who does not each have an advantage. So from common-sense confusion, research produces a general, complex, precise statement of the nature and amount of the effect of government spending on voting and the *limits of scope* of that effect. Concern with a specific election, which is the common-sense approach, could never yield this rich result.

Note, too, from this example that the terms employed—"marginal difference," "broaden a coalition"—are more remote from daily experience than the original common-sense terms. Like "mass," "evolution," and "electrons," such terms sensitize us to features of the world which we would ordinarily not notice or unite objects and findings which would seem to be unrelated. Before Newton, who could see links between apples falling, tides rising, and planets revolving around the sun? Since Newton's conception of "mass" and his universal law of gravitation, who could *fail* to see them? In social science, concepts like "reference group," "relative deprivation," and "defensiveness" have had such effects.

Social science research also expands perception by formulating problems and solutions which are beyond the pale of common sense. A nonliterate culture may see a problem as "evil spirits" or "angered ancestors," rather than "social deviance" or "social conflict." An industrialized culture may have an equally limited view of problems, as when racial conflict is solely blamed on unemployed ghetto residents. Or a husband and wife each blame the other for their marital dissatisfaction, instead of viewing their *relationship* as a faltering partnership, or even viewing the institution of marriage as one which has come under excessive demands.

Common sense formulates neither theoretical nor methodological problems, since it takes its assumptions and methods as given. Thus, it is not commonsensical to ask, as social scientists have, what are the consequences of alienation, depersonalization, inflation, and underemployment, for the stability of our current political system? For its responsiveness? For the individual personality? Nor is it possible to ask in a commonsensical way to what extent "years of formal education" adequately reflect the theoretical concept "education." Such questions simply do not come up. Consequently, common-sense problems and solutions are self-limited. To avoid research in order to be "relevant" might thus perpetuate useless or incomplete ways of thinking about problems. There is nothing so practical ("relevant") as a good, explicit theory and trustworthy, explicit ways of testing it.

Underlying the above comparisons is a recognition that social science research relies on the scientific method. While we will consider the logic behind the scientific method in detail in Chapter 2, at this point we note the *cyclical* nature of this approach. Like common sense, the scientific method begins with facts, but it then progresses through theories and predictions, and returns to new facts that form the end of one cycle and the beginning of the next (Oskamp, 1972). If observed facts are used to generate a theory consistent with the facts, the process is called *induction*— the first step in the scientific method. The second step is *deduction*. Here

induction

deduction

we ask what are the consequences of the theory? What specific implications does our general theory reflect? The act of collecting new facts which permit us to decide whether the theory is supported or refuted is the third

verification   step, called *verification*. Usually these new findings cause us to modify the theory at least (if not reject it), leading thus to a new cycle of induction, deduction, and verification (Oskamp, 1972).

One of the functions of social research is to develop and evaluate practices, concepts, and theories of social relations and to develop and evaluate methodologies that test these practices, concepts, and theories—in short, to know the limits of one's knowledge and keep pressing against them. Yet social research may be entirely *practical* in its function; the desire may be to know for the sake of being able to do something better or more efficiently. We consider these uses in the next section.

II. SOME SOCIAL USES OF SOCIAL RESEARCH

Unfortunately, the bulk of social science research is done without the intention of making practical applications. What, then, are the applied uses of social research? The most general answer, of course, is to improve the quality of social life. There are several ways to do this. One is to give decision makers substantive advice about what to decide. Such advice is given to public policy makers, as when psychologists are called upon by the police to help prevent a riot; to private policy makers, as when a telephone manufacturing company asks a team of sociologists to help them increase plant efficiency (Roethlisberger and Dickson, 1939); and to individual decision makers (and potential or actual policy makers), as when a social scientist writes a book describing how to change people's attitudes toward the Vietnam war (Rosenberg, *et al.*, 1970).

At times, the advice is wise and is taken seriously. A trend-setting example of applied social research was accomplished by the Research Branch of the Information and Education Division of the U.S. Department of War during World War II (Stouffer, *et al.*, 1949):

> The Research Branch existed to do a practical engineering job, not a scientific job. Its purpose was to provide the Army command quickly and accurately with facts about the attitudes of soldiers which, along with other facts and inferences, might be helpful in policy formation (Vol. I, p. 5).

The Research Branch did many small engineering jobs (most of which had no direct payoff for social science), such as finding out why soldiers did not use as much Atabrine as the army wished; finding out preferences for kinds of huts in Alaska, winter clothing in Europe, radio programs, and articles in *Yank* magazine; and assessing needs for different kinds of athletic equipment.

But some of the projects dealt squarely with major army-wide problems.

To name a few: developing a psychoneurotic inventory used at all United States induction stations; raising morale through revision of the pay scale and the development of a publicity program; planning for the redistribution of overseas returnees; publishing regularly a practical summary of current research findings for officers, emphasizing "problems which were susceptible to treatment at the local command level" (Stouffer, et al., 1949, Vol. I, p. 10); developing and testing war orientation films; and, perhaps most important of all, establishing the criteria and priorities by which the armed forces were demobilized after the war.

The work of the Research Branch has also had great impact on the development of social science research, both substantive and methodological. In the former there are new findings and ideas about primary groups, reference groups, relative deprivation, and persuasion, to name a few. In the latter there are statistical elaboration, Guttman scaling, latent structure analysis, and controlled experimentation. Indeed, the face of social science would probably be very different today without the efforts and achievements of the Research Branch.

Research need not be applied intentionally to current events to be relevant to them. John Maynard Keynes's economic theories, C. Wright Mills's concept of the "military-industrial complex," and John Kenneth Galbraith's concept of "techno-structure," to name a few, have influenced the thought patterns and expectations of national policy makers in the United States. Yet, none was developed intentionally for them. Similarly, studies of the development of various nations have been used to brief U.S. State and Defense Department officials, without having been done for them. And, most familiar to Americans, when the U.S. Supreme Court declared racial segregation in public schools unconstitutional (in *Brown* v. *Board of Education*, 1954), its finding was based in part on several social science studies, none of which had originally been prepared for the legal case. As Horowitz (1971) has said: "[P]olicy-making may prove to be less dependent upon policy-makers than upon the general intellectual productions of a given epoch" (p. 8).

In any case, there are many indications that social science advice on policy and programs is in great and increasing demand. For instance:

> Most federal programs in the field of "human resources" are currently demanding evaluation of program outcomes, and . . . they are providing large sums of money for large-scale studies. A recent review of only *federally* funded evaluations with budgets in excess of $25,000 turned up approximately a thousand such studies in one year (1970) (Weiss, 1972, pp. xi–xii).

But this can get out of hand. There is a danger that social science research findings may be used to justify the support of existing social practices that exploit those limited in power. (For example, invalid IQ test results can be used to keep children from different cultural backgrounds in "special" classes.) It is also the case that the major funds for financing most research come from government, the military, business, and foundations—in other words, institutions that represent the interests of certain groups more than others.

Policy advice is most useful as "applied science" when there is a science to apply. Likewise, Dr. Joyce Brothers must have a constant production of new knowledge before she can respond to new inquiries about personal problems. That is, without a wealth of well-tested theories, social scientists risk basing their advice on advocacy or personal opinion rather than on expertise. In the absence of trustworthy empirical evidence, the policy maker is likely to be guided by political pressure. And it may be effective policy, too, since there will probably be more local-citizen support for its implementation. Of course, some policy makers and followers of Dr. Joyce Brothers will ignore the expert's advice anyway, for there are numerous reasons that discourage them from basing their decisions on research. In order to enact a policy, one has to advocate it with confidence that it will work. Rigorous evaluation of policy effectiveness thus entails great political **overadvocacy** risk. Aside from this "overadvocacy trap" (Campbell, 1969b) there are **trap** other reasons why research is not used in policy formation: ordinary organizational resistance to change, lack of resources to implement recommendations, and various inadequacies in the conduct and presentation of researchers' recommendations (Weiss, 1972).

The advice of social scientists as a basis for decision making may be particularly odious when there is no reliable body of knowledge on which to base expertise. The "experts" then make judgments that are often not superior to those of the layman or politician. And they must expend considerable resources to maintain the facade of expertise. Needless jargon, unduly complicated formulas, and confinement of research to investigation which lacks directly observable significant consequences, after all, are troublesome to all, but more so to "outsiders," for they are constructed to keep them outside. A social science "priesthood" develops.

For instance, Operation Head Start was evaluated in a careless way which falsely made this educational intervention program appear harmful (Campbell and Erlebacher, 1970). Where reliable information is lacking, one's own sensitivity and empathy are often more valuable in decision making than is willingness to follow the judgments of "experts." And it is precisely because there are great gaps in contemporary social science knowledge, which are somehow not matched by the modesty of claims among social scientists, that policy makers, parents, car purchasers, and all of us *must* be able to make researchers demonstrate their claims according to the canons of science and scholarship.

The fact is that evaluation research *is* being done, much of it by federally funded agencies as required by law. To ignore the importance of research in current United States domestic policy, then, is to ignore some possibilities for policy impact. For the student who wants to have an impact on the administration of social services, the great and increasing demand (Weiss, 1972) for conductors of evaluation research affords an excellent opportunity. And for the administrator, evaluation research managed properly can increase organizational effectiveness.

To avoid the "overadvocacy" and "priesthood" traps among social researchers, Campbell (1971) emphasized for the social researcher

> . . . the more passive role . . . as an aid in helping society decide whether or not its innovations have achieved desired goals without damaging side effects. The job of the methodologist for the experimenting society is not to say *what is to be done*, but rather to say *what has been done*. The aspect of social science that is being applied is primarily its research methodology rather than its descriptive theory, with the goal of learning more than we do now from the innovations decided upon by the political process (p. 8).

For social science has not yet achieved the knowledge necessary for reliable advice on the content of policy:

> We have no elegantly successful theories that predict precisely in widely different settings. Nor do we have the capacity to make definitive choices among competing theories. Even if we had, the social settings of ameliorative programs involve so many complexities that the guesses of the experienced administrator and politician are apt to be on the average as wise as those of social scientists. But whatever the source of the implemented guess, we learn only by checking it out (Campbell, 1971, p. 8).

The evaluation of programs is, of course, a direct application of scientific testing procedures—the research attitude—to social policy. It removes policy from unsystematic, test-resistant common sense.

One further use of social research in seeking the improvement of the quality of life is to develop measures of the quality of life. This is another perception-expanding device, for the resulting "social indicators" (Bauer, 1966; Bell, 1969; Campbell and Converse, 1972; Sheldon and Moore, 1968; U.S. Department of Health, Education and Welfare, 1969) can be used to generate data useful for testing new theories as well as for evaluating programs according to specified purposes. Lacking such indicators, we must either let policy drift or else evaluate it according to those goals for which we already have measures available. The latter course would restrict us to preexisting goals, to common-sense problems in whose terms (usually economic, like Gross National Product) such data have been previously gathered.

The application of research to social problems may raise as many problems as it solves. But, as Campbell (1971) pointed out, that possibility, too, must be rigorously evaluated by social research.

III. THE VALUE OF UNDERSTANDING THE RESEARCH PROCESS

Even though research may raise as many questions as it answers, there remains a constant effort to devise procedures that will increase the probable accuracy of research answers. Why is it important to be familiar with the research process? For the student who is preparing for a career of carrying out research in social psychology, political science, marketing, or sociology, the answer is obvious: Research techniques are the tools of the trade. The student needs not only to develop skill in using them but also to understand the logic behind them.

But it is not only the student who intends to carry out research who needs to know about research methods. The positions for which social science students are likely to be preparing themselves—teaching, administration in government or business, community consultation, social work—increasingly call for the ability to evaluate and to use research results: to judge whether a study has been carried out in such a way that one can have reasonable confidence in its findings and whether its findings are applicable to the specific situation at hand.

Even if one does not expect to make specific use of research findings in his or her job, in our scientific age all of us are in many ways "consumers" of research results. To use them intelligently, we need to be able to judge the adequacy of the methods by which they have been obtained. As a student, for example, you will find that many of the "facts" presented in your courses rest on the results of research. But you may discover that the "facts" reported by one study are quite different from those produced by another study on the same point. One investigator, for example, may report that children who are weaned early grow up to be more independent and better adjusted than those who are nursed for a longer time; another investigator turns up with just the opposite finding. Or several studies may conclude that when Blacks and whites live near each other, each group is likely to become more favorably inclined toward the other; but other studies may conclude that interracial hostility is likely to be especially intense in neighborhoods where Blacks and whites live in close proximity. In order to be able to make a tentative judgment about which conclusion merits more confidence, you need to be able to judge the adequacy of the studies. Later sections of this book will consider the criteria of good research in detail. Here we may suggest simply that you will want to ask such questions as: How do the investigators define their terms? Are they really both talking about the same things, or have they used the same words for different phenomena? Was the evidence they gathered relevant to the problem? Were there any obvious sources of bias in the way the data were gathered? Were there different conditions in the studies that might account for the difference in findings?

Even in the course of daily living, the average citizen increasingly needs to be able to evaluate research in order to make intelligent decisions. This is perhaps most clear with respect to medical research and decisions based on it: Should I have my child inoculated with influenza vaccine? Should I move out of the city because of the dangers of industrial pollution? Should I stop smoking in order to lessen the risk of getting lung cancer? With the rapid increase in social science research, it seems likely that the average citizen will increasingly be presented with social findings. As we indicated in the previous section, at the present time the citizen has relatively little occasion to evaluate these findings as a basis for his or her own actions. But the person who knows how research is carried out is better able to judge the probable accuracy of opinion polls or election predictions and to view with appropriate skepticism the claims that "nine doctors out of ten approve. . . ."

Besides all these practical advantages of familiarity with research methods, there is the satisfaction of acquiring a new intellectual tool. And it is a tool with much broader uses than the specific purposes for which it was devised. It can become a way of looking at the world, of judging everyday experience. People who really understand the basic elements of research method are in a position to ask, with respect to every statement they read or hear: What is the basis for that view? Is it supported by evidence? Under what conditions is it likely to hold true? Of course, they will not necessarily question all statements in this way. As has already been pointed out, not all matters are appropriately considered in this way. If friends admire a beautiful sunset, or express a preference for spending their vacation in the mountains, it is irrelevant to question the factual basis or the "objective truth" of their opinion. It may often be inappropriate to change the tone of a social situation by demanding evidence for a statement lightly made. But if one reads that public opinion, as reflected in mail to members of Congress, is opposed to foreign aid, or that a legislator has proposed curing juvenile delinquency by fining the parents of delinquents, or if one hears neighbors say that they will not sell their home to a Puerto Rican family because it would spoil the neighborhood—one may well want to raise, at least in one's own mind, such questions as: How do you know that? What are the facts on which you base your conclusion? Is the interpretation warranted by the facts?

IV. MAJOR STEPS IN RESEARCH

The object of this book is to describe in detail the procedures necessary to discover answers to questions through research. But since concern with detail often obscures perception of the whole, it is well, before embarking on the examination of specific procedures, to point out some over-all aspects of the research process.

The research process consists of a number of closely related activities that overlap continuously rather than follow a strictly prescribed sequence. So interdependent are these activities that the first step of a research project largely determines the nature of the last. If subsequent procedures have not been taken into account in the early stages, serious difficulties may arise and prevent the completion of a study. *Frequently these difficulties cannot be remedied at the time they become apparent because they are rooted in the earlier procedures.* They can be avoided only by keeping in mind, at each step of the research process, the requirements of subsequent steps.

To be sure, as research proceeds from the conception of a theme for a study through the gathering of data to the production of a report and the application of the findings, the focus of attention will necessarily shift from one activity to the next. This shift reflects a difference in emphasis, however, rather than an exclusive concentration on an isolated step. A mechanically consecutive sequence of procedures, in which one research step is entirely completed before the next is begun, is rarely, if ever, the experience of social scientists.

The usual pattern of *reporting* research creates an oversimplified expectation of what is involved in *doing* research. Customarily, a report on completed research, when it appears as an article in a technical journal, resembles, with minor modifications, the following model.

1. A statement of purpose is made in the form of *formulating the problem.*
2. A description of the *study design* is given.
3. The *methods of data collection* are specified.
4. The *results* are presented.
5. Frequently, there follows a section on *conclusions and interpretation* (usually called the Discussion Section).

Whatever the individual variations from this model, published research strongly suggests the existence of a prescribed sequence of procedures, each step presupposing the completion of the preceding one. Although this model is entirely justified in the interest of economy of scientific reporting, it must not be mistaken for a model of the research process, which differs from it in two respects. The research process almost never follows the neat sequential pattern of activities suggested in the organization of research reports, and the process involves many additional activities which are rarely mentioned in published studies (Hammond, 1964).

Some of these additional activities are related to the scientific requirements of the study, others to its practical demands. The apparently simple reporting of the methods of data collection, for example, summarizes decisions about the kinds of data needed and the most efficient way of collecting them, and the activities carried out in the development and pretesting of the data-collection instruments. In addition to these steps, related to the scientific requirements of the study, there are other, more practical, demands: the budget must be planned; funds must be obtained and administered; personnel must be allocated and, in some cases, specially trained; the setting within which the data are to be collected must be explored and the cooperation of the people in it must be gained; and so on. In addition, if the study is one designed to solve an immediate, practical problem, the anticipated application of the findings must be considered from the outset.

V. ORGANIZATION OF THE TEXT

This book describes the major steps in the process of social research. The demands of organization require that these steps be discussed separately and consecutively, but it should always be kept in mind that the steps are not so clearly demarcated from one another as an organized discussion makes them appear to be.

Chapter 2 evaluates the logic underlying a scientific analysis. Chapter 3 discusses the problems and considerations arising in the selection and formulation of a research question. Chapters 4 and 5 deal with research design and its functions in a scientific inquiry. Variations in design are discussed, from the relatively unstructured exploration of a problem to the rigorous testing of hypotheses by means of controlled experiments.

Chapter 6 describes reliability and validity and presents some general problems of measurement in the social sciences, providing a background for later chapters. Chapter 7 discusses the ethical questions in social research to be considered before beginning collection of data. Chapters 8, 9, and 10 consider three broad groups of data-collection methods—observational methods, questionnaires and interviews, and projective techniques. Chapter 11 treats the use of data already available, such as archival and statistical records and the content of communications and personal documents. Chapter 12 discusses techniques for placing individuals on scales on the basis of data collected by any of the methods considered in the preceding chapters.

Chapter 13 deals with the rapidly developing field of data processing; Chapter 14 with the analysis and interpretation of data; and finally, Chapter 15 with the writing of a research report.

chapter

THE LOGIC
OF ANALYSIS

I. INTRODUCTION

Science involves many things—theory, technique, method, and apparatus, to name just a few. But it is particularly useful to speak of science in terms which reflect some of the things that scientists do as well as some of the more formal views of science.

Science can be thought of as a strategy for explanation. Social scientists are particularly concerned with explaining why events occur and why people behave as they do. Social scientists try to describe and explain social and individual processes so that events can be understood. Once the dynamics of an event are understood, it is then possible to predict such an event. Sometimes it is possible to control occurrences of similar events. Why do racial riots occur? What can be done about these causes? What impact will specific actions have both on racial uprisings and on other areas of society at the same time?

In advancing explanations and descriptions of events, scientists do three kinds of things: They exercise imagination and creative insight; they perform logical analysis; and they make judgments that are based on observations of the events that they wish to explain.

A. Developing theories through imagination and insight

theory　It will be helpful to clarify exactly what we mean by a theory. A *theory* is a set of concepts plus the interrelationships that are assumed to exist among those concepts. A theory also includes consequences that we assume logically to follow from the relationships proposed in the theory. These consequences are called hypotheses.

Concepts are terms that refer to the characteristics of events, situations, groups, and individuals that we are studying in the social sciences. Some typical concepts include "race," "moral maturity," "political party preference," and "pessimism." Indeed, it is reference to concepts like these that ties scientific theories to the world of observation. Concepts are linked to each other by logical words to form relationships. We may propose, for example, that Blacks are "more pessimistic" than whites. The theory behind this proposition would deal with reasons for relationships between a social characteristic such as race and an internal state of pessimism.

hypotheses *Hypotheses*, or the consequences of our theoretical assumptions, are the statements that we usually submit to actual testing. Hypotheses are empirically tested because we are uncertain of the extent to which they are correct. Hypotheses logically follow from a theory—indeed, a theory can be viewed as a set of reasons why a hypothesis should be true. Most social science theories assume the form that if X, Y, and Z are true, then A most likely is also true because A tends to follow from X, Y, and Z.

For example, let us say that a theory assumes that mass media lead poor people to acquire a desire for those possessions that they have not had before. Furthermore, the theory proposes that, because of job discrimination, it is not possible to obtain these possessions through socially approved means (such as earning enough money to purchase the goods), and that the desire for the possessions creates frustrations, and that frustrations lead to the behavior of participating in a riot. Then one hypothesis that would follow from the preceding assumptions is that exposure to the media is related to the incidence of riots (Gurr, 1970). In this particular example, X, Y, and Z are assumptions and A is the hypothesis which logically follows: that exposure to media leads to rioting.

Social science theories are rarely elegant or sophisticated. In fact, social science theories usually assume the form of a series of assumptions that are loosely tied together and seem to lead to hypotheses. The point we wish to emphasize is that one should be able to understand what the assumptions, concepts, and hypotheses of the theory are as presented in social science writing. If assumptions, concepts, and hypotheses in a study cannot be identified, then we question the extent to which this study satisfies minimal standards of science.

Scientists create theories and scientists test hypotheses. Some social scientists may emphasize creating theories while others emphasize testing them, but neither creating theory nor testing theory can advance very well in isolation from each other. In this chapter, we discuss general aspects of theory development and testing that apply to science in general and to social science in particular.

Thus, we talk about the kinds of things scientists do and the kinds of concerns they have while doing it. Although the following material gives the appearance of a fairly orderly series of activities and processes, the reader must not assume that science involves a fixed or predictable sequence of tasks and concerns. (This is particularly true when discussing scientific theorizing, a form of creativity which involves several tasks and concerns at the same time.) It may be easier to understand a neatly organized discussion of science, but it is not feasible to do science by rote even if it were desirable. Scientists present their findings in a systematic and standard way, suggesting to some that the actual work and thinking that lies behind the written account was performed in a mechanical manner. Such standard formats are used for purposes of clarity rather than as descriptions of creative thinking about scientific problems.

Theory building involves imagination that is exercised in a particularly rigorous way. Theory is an intellectual creation; scientific theories await invention, not discovery. The assumptions on which theories are based require human ingenuity.

But the fecundity of hypotheses and the ways in which they are tested also depend greatly on the inventiveness of the analyst. So, too, do the final formulations of social science theories and hypotheses. What makes this type of scientific creativity particularly difficult and exciting is the requirement that the assumptions and hypotheses of social science theories confront the world as human beings perceive it.

B. Logical analysis, in the ideal sense

Science also involves the use of logic for inference and analysis. Logical analysis is concerned with the relationship between a conclusion and the evidence given to support it. Inference is reasoning from one set of beliefs to a second set. If the inference is made verbally, then it becomes an "argument" (as that word is used in the technical terminology of logic). If an inference is not made explicit—if it is not transformed into an "argument"—then it cannot be subjected to logical analysis. It then remains a conclusion that is without evidence, and we cannot say it is a logical inference (Salmon, 1966). Logic, then, concerns the strength of the evidence linking the premises and conclusions of arguments (Skyrms, 1966). Logic is not concerned with the truth or falsity of individual premises. A logically correct argument may contain false premises. But in a logically correct argument, *if* the premises are true, then there are good grounds for accepting the conclusion as true.

Two different criteria of logical correctness are applied to arguments: deductive validity and inductive strength. Recall that deduction and induction were introduced in Chapter 1. *Deductive validity* deals with the relationship of premises to conclusion: if and only if the premises are true, the conclusion must be true. The truth of the premises guarantees the truth of the conclusion, when deductive validity is the consideration. In a deductive argument, it is impossible for the conclusion to be false while the premises are true. This is because all of the factual information in the conclusion is already contained (at least implicitly) in the premises. For example:

Premises	1. In all organizations, the many are dominated by the few.
	2. All religious groups are organizations.
Conclusion	3. In all religious groups, the many are dominated by the few.

The only way in which religious groups could not be "dominated by the few" is if they are not organizations or if not all organizations are dominated by the few. We could not possibly imagine a situation in which statement 3 is false while the first two are true. This is because statement 3 is already contained in the first two. This can most readily be seen by drawing a diagram (Figure 2.1) to represent the first two statements. S, the square, represents all situations where the few dominate the many; O, the circle, represents all organizations; and P, the triangle, represents all religious groups. According to premise 1, O is in S. According to premise 2, P is in O. And, *without drawing another line*, we see that P is in S. There is no way to draw this diagram faithfully without placing P in S; that placement is implicit in the premises. Note here that neither premise need be true for the argument to be deductively valid.

Since the truth of individual statements is independent of the logical correctness of the arguments they form, *it is possible to infer a true conclusion from either true or false premises*. One can be right for the wrong reasons. For instance:

Premises	1. All New York citizens are Martians.
	2. All Martians are United States citizens.
Conclusion	3. All New York citizens are United States citizens.

This is a deductively valid argument with false premises and a true conclusion.

In science, we reason from theories (premises) to hypotheses (conclusions), but we can examine the truth of only the hypotheses. Clearly, it

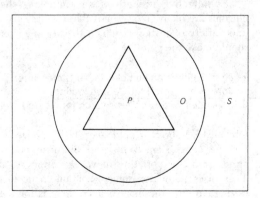

FIGURE 2.1 Diagram of deductive validity.

would be erroneous to infer the truth of hypotheses. Alternate theories could produce the same hypothesis. We can say about a theory whose hypothesis is true the following: that the theory had an opportunity to be shown false, and failed to be rejected. However, if the conclusions (hypotheses) are false in a deductively valid argument, then the theories must be false. In deductively valid arguments, true premises *guarantee* true conclusions. If the conclusion is false, then the premises cannot all be true.

Deductive validity is a logical criterion applied in science to relationships between theoretical statements and in linking theories to hypotheses, whose observable truth or falsity provides an estimate of the theory's truth or falsity.

In contrast, an argument can be *inductively strong* even if it is not deductively valid. In the case of *inductive validity*, when all the premises are true, the conclusion is probably true. It is only probable because the conclusion makes claims beyond those of the premises. For example:

Premise	1. In all religious groups observed so far, the many are dominated by the few.
Conclusion	2. In all religious groups, the many are dominated by the few.

The conclusion here is not necessarily true even if the premise is. Tomorrow we might find a nonoligarchical religious group. But since we never have, we probably never will. While the premise refers to groups observed so far, the conclusion goes beyond that to cover religions not yet observed. Since the conclusion contains information the premise does not, its truth is not guaranteed by the truth of the premise. We make an "inductive leap" from premise to conclusion and risk falling into the gap between them.

Whereas an argument is either deductively valid or invalid, it may have varying degrees of inductive strength, depending on how well the premises support the conclusion.

The inductive strength of an argument—the extent to which the conclusions are likely to be true if the premises are—increases with the number and variety of instances which the argument embodies. A simple example should make the point:

Premises	1. John Smith is an eligible United States voter.
	2. John Smith voted for George Wallace.
Conclusion	3. All United States citizens voted for George Wallace.

Obviously, nobody would accept the above premises as strong evidence for the conclusion. Why not? Because one case (Smith) provides no opportunity for variation in voting. Suppose, then, we add another case. Two cases allow for some variation to occur, but not much. The more cases there are, the more chance there is for the conclusion to change and, consequently, the more persuasive would be its failure to change. The number of cases needed to support a conclusion depends on the particular problem. However, it is clear that "jumping to conclusions" is inductively weak argumentation.

Suppose we have a sample of one million United States voters, most of whom voted for George Wallace. Is that strong evidence that most United States voters did so? That depends on how the million were selected. If they are all white Southerners, then the argument is weak, for white Southerners have been more likely than other Unied States citizens to vote for Wallace. The *variety* of instances, then, increases the inductive strength of an argument: the more different kinds of instances there are, the more likely it is that conclusions are not limited to a particular, unrepresentative kind.

C. The actual situation, as opposed to the ideal

Hypotheses (or propositions) are generalizations that follow from the assumptions that are embedded in a theory, as we indicated above. The validity, or the logical correctness, of the relationship between hypotheses and assumptions in theories is a matter of obvious concern. Do the hypotheses *really* follow from the theory as stated or not? To what extent are hypotheses that have been derived from a theory consistent with each other? To what extent do the hypotheses contradict others?

Ambiguity is a major foe of logical consistency and also of understanding. Ambiguity exists whenever the concepts present in theories and hypotheses can have more than one meaning. One does not know exactly what a concept means, so that interpretation of hypotheses in which the concept appears is likely to be different at different times and for different people. What does *alienation* mean, for example? Certainly, if we do not know what we are talking about in using a concept, it is unlikely that we will use the concept in the same way on repeated occasions. And it is still less likely that anyone else will use it in the same way. Communication and logic then suffer.

Many of the words that appear in social science theories are words that also have meanings in the society in which we live. Sometimes these meanings are unclear. Sometimes they vary greatly from one subculture to another within the society. Frequently—in the case of words like *race* or *authoritarian*—highly charged emotional meanings blur meanings that social scientists wish to ascribe to concepts. It is necessary to clarify the precise ways in which such concepts are used, if we are to communicate accurately with each other.

Inconsistencies may also be introduced by lack of care in making formulations, or by failure to consider thoroughly the implications of generalizations. Careful analysis of the logic in the theories is necessary in order to root out inconsistencies which may be introduced in these ways.

The meanings of many terms, particularly in the social sciences, may also be far from clear. Careful analysis is useful in specifying what is and what is not included in the meaning of theoretical concepts. Exactly what kinds of characteristics are included as defining a concept? What characteristics are similar to these, but are not included in the definition and may therefore lead to confusion? What are the different ways the concept has been used? Are there different consequences for the different uses of concepts? What are they? Why? Does a given term apply in all situations or only in some situations? If a term applies in only a few situations, then which situations are those? Are there any others?

D. Observation and evidence

empiricism Finally, science is based on empiricism. By the term *empiricism*, we simply mean that evidence that originates directly *or indirectly* through normal human senses is admissible as support for or against a hypothesis, but that no other kind of evidence counts. These senses include sight, taste, touch, hearing, and smell. All humans whose physiological equipment functions normally are able to see, taste, feel, hear, or smell stimuli of kinds that can be specified and under conditions which can be specified. People can see a baseball, for example, but they cannot see a neutron. But people can see neutrons indirectly, by observing photographic representations of paths neutrons leave. Under no normal conditions can people regularly observe ghosts. Nor do ghosts leave any other observable or tangible manifestations. Thus, we can have scientific theories about baseballs and neutrons but not about ghosts.

This does not deny that other theories of knowing (called epistemologies) exist and may be valid; rather, the argument asserts that as far as scientific knowledge is concerned, only empirically based evidence counts. We are not denying that other ways of knowing may exist. Many religions, for example, identify revelation (a special, nonempirical, individual way of finding things out) as a source of knowledge. Intuition, visions, and reflective thought are all nonempirical strategies for acquiring knowledge about the social and physical worlds, since not all persons with normal sensory equipment will "discover" the same thing when following these strategies. But one cannot use information gained from these ways of finding out as scientific evidence for or against hypotheses and theories.

Thus, for science all evidence used for theories must come originally from the senses, and it must be possible for any person who has the normal sensory equipment (functioning in the normal way) to be able to make the same observations. Others need to be able to replicate observations that an investigator makes. And if others cannot replicate observations under normal conditions, then serious questions must be raised about the evidence used in a study. Great importance is placed on fully describing the way a study is conducted, so that others can attempt to replicate its observations.

II. THEORIZING

Theorizing is the process of creating and developing theory. As we have viewed theory in the above discussion, this means creating and developing explanations about social behavior. In this section, we outline what an explanation is and discuss the role of conceptual analysis and theoretical elaboration in theorizing. We introduce what is a new term for many **retroduction** readers, "retroduction," to describe another process used in scientific explanation.

A. Explanations

One may wonder why one senatorial candidate wins while another loses, or why some people drink alcohol to excess while others drink only moderately and still others drink not at all, or why prices vary in seasonal patterns, or why protests by mistreated racial groups occur only at certain times and not at others, or why a variety of events occur in a number of social arenas. Theorizing is mainly a process of inventing sets of reasons to account for such events (Stinchcombe, 1968).

Scientists try to explain events. And explanations employ theories that relate ideas we have to observations that we make. We set up a series of assumptions about aspects of the social world which we then relate to what it is we wish to explain. When we have demonstrated that a series of logically interrelated assumptions lead to a conclusion, we have explained the event (Hempel, 1966). The explanation is primarily a set of reasons why the event occurred the way that it did. A more extensive discussion of the components of an explanation will be helpful.

A scientific explanation has one or more generalizations, one or more specific observations and a conclusion. The generalizations are assumptions about some recurrent feature of social behavior. It is important to note that whatever body of theory—that is, an interrelated set of assumptions—one has about the event to be explained is included in the generalizations. Each generalization contains specific concepts which represent characteristics (or properties) of events with which we are concerned. The concepts are related to each other in each generalization by logical phrases which imply association or dissociation. The most common phrases linking concepts are "if x, then y," "if x, then not y," "x causes y," "x leads to y," or "x and y tend to go together," where x and y are concepts. Although generalizations are usually about a certain group of events, they are to be understood as *general* in the sense that they are assumed to be about more than specific observations of the events to which they are being applied in any given study.

Finally, explanations include conclusions. Conclusions are statements about the relationship between the behaviors we have observed and wish to explain. These conclusions logically follow from our generalizations together with our specific observations.

B. A reconstructed explanation

For the sake of clarity, let us reconstruct one explanation. In discussing why some people participate in urban riots and others do not, Fogelson and Hill (1968) outlined what they called the "riffraff theory" of riot participation (which the authors later questioned severely in their study of the 1967 Detroit urban riots). A presentation of this ill-advised riffraff theory follows.

The so-called riffraff comprise an extremely tough, highly transient, poor group of people who are not adequately socialized into the norms of the community. Nonriffraff, in contrast, have learned community norms and tend to be stable residents of the community. Community norms oppose illegal activities and especially illegal activities for personal gain. Urban riots offer an opportunity for personal gain and are also illegal. Riffraff participate in riots—the theory proposes—while nonriffraff oppose riots or at least do not actively participate in them. Nonriffraff comprise the vast majority of the population. A schematic presentation of the riffraff theory which explains the participation of the riffraff in urban riots would be:

Generalization
1. People who do not hold strong community norms engage in illegal activities for personal gain.
2. People who hold strong community norms avoid engaging in illegal activity for personal gain and actively oppose illegal activity for personal gain.

Observations
3. Riots are illegal but may result in personal gain for participants.
4. Riffraff do not hold strong community norms.
5. Nonriffraff hold strong community norms.

Conclusions
6. Riffraff would tend to participate in riots.
7. Nonriffraff would avoid participation in riots.
8. Nonriffraff would oppose participation in riots.

We wish to explain why certain persons participate in urban riots and why others do not. The generalizations in the above explanation provide reasons why some kinds of people (riffraff) would engage in illegal activities for personal gain and why other people (nonriffraff) would not engage in illegal activity for personal gain. Since a riot is an illegal activity that can lead to personal gain, the theory expected that riffraff would engage in rioting, and that nonriffraff would avoid such behavior.

When asked, "Why would riffraff participate in riots?" one can say *because* riffraff are not constrained by community norms of behavior. Similarly, nonriffraff do not engage in rioting *because* nonriffraff *are* constrained by community norms of behavior. Thus, the presence or absence of community norms of behavior in two social groups *explains why* one group participates in the behavior of rioting and the other group does not. Once we have answered "why," we have explained the behavior in question.

The riffraff theory of behavior in riots may not be a correct explanation. That is, it may not be empirically valid. The matter of testing empirical validity will be dealt with later in this chapter and other places in this book. The riffraff theory may not, moreover, be a very adequate explanation in the sense that it does not enable highly accurate or precise predictions of individual participation or even of which cities will have urban riots. The question of adequacy also will be discussed below. Although it may not be correct and it may not be valid, the riffraff theory of riots qualifies as one scientific explanation, among many.

People who do not hold strong community norms are assumed to be more likely to engage in rioting not only in the Detroit ghetto, but at any place in which the condition of undersocialization exists as well. People who are well socialized concerning community norms are assumed to *avoid* rioting not only in Detroit but also in other communities. Finally, the behavior of rioting is only one type of illegal activity in which riffraff could participate. The theory suggests that riffraff would engage in other illegal but profitable activities as well. This *generalization* and the body of theory from which it is derived are general with respect to the specific individuals, groups, and conditions that are covered, as well as with respect to the specific forms of deviance that are concerned.

The *specific observations* that have a part in explanations are the particular characteristics of events that make the generalizations relevant to what we are trying to explain. In the case of participation in urban riots, for example, it is necessary to show that community norms are less well ingrained among those who are participating in the riot than those who are not, and that the riot situation is one in which participants and non-participants alike perceive a chance to make personal gain out of the chaos. Otherwise, the generalization is not relevant to the behavior we wish to explain.

If we wish to explain an event, we do not use generalizations that contain irrelevant concepts. It is necessary, therefore, to demonstrate the application and relevance of each concept to the specific observations concerning the events we explain in order to make the generalizations in our explanation relevant to the conclusion.

Finally, the *conclusion* in this explanation is what all this analysis leads to. People participate in rioting *because* they are not well socialized into community norms. When we can demonstrate *how* generalizations and observations lead logically to conclusions, we have *explained* an event. And this is all that can be expected of a scientific explanation, despite whatever additional criteria we might wish to apply to scientific theories.

When theorizing, one should make explicit the generalizations, specific observations, and conclusions. We cannot overemphasize the point that creating explanations in the pursuit of theory is a process of invention. This process of invention is made clearer if we understand precisely what we are discussing and thinking about. Explicit use of concepts, interrelationships between concepts, and specific observations to which concepts apply—all these aid the process of invention by clarifying what may be fruitful or fruitless, consistent or contradictory.

C. Inventing explanations

Theorists do two major kinds of things in inventing explanations. One of these is to look at what other invesigators say about the phenomenon they are studying. Looking at what others say gives them ideas about constructing explanations that might not have otherwise come to mind. Looking at what others say also informs them about the extent of evidence for particular explanations. It is particularly important in this regard to consider explanations that are plausible and that offer alternatives to the explanation one has in mind.

In the study of the Detroit riot, for instance, Fogelson and Hill observed that although many public officials disagreed on the causes of riots in specific cities and the issues which undergird various riots, the public officials tended to agree as to which types of citizens participated in the riots. Most officials believed that participants in the racial disorders were primarily the riffraff.

Had Fogelson and Hill accepted this near consensus as an accurate description of the constituency of the riot participants, there would have been little point in continuing the study. But they observed that other explanations existed. The chief plausible alternative explanation had to do with the impact of discrimination on the *entire* Black community from which certain people chose to riot (Fogelson and Hill, 1968). This view suggested the hypothesis that participation in urban riots might be more widespread and more representative of the Black community than the riffraff theory suggested. This explanation proposed that Blacks rioted because anger generated by discriminatory treatment was great. A second very plausible alternative explanation was that a variety of systematic errors biased records of arrests, so that the riffraff theory only *appeared* to be correct. Conclusions based on arrest records overemphasized the indigent, and transient Blacks because they were more likely than higher-status Blacks to be arrested and detained. This explanation was based on evidence and knowledge about discrimination by the police in arresting lower-status Blacks.

As a second way of inventing explanations, theorists observe characteristics of the events under study in order to try to generalize "from the data." The search is for similarities and differences in concepts that occur in the presence or in the absence of what we are trying to explain. Whenever X occurs, does Y also occur? Whenever Z occurs, is Y always absent? Does Y occur only in the presence of W, but never in its absence? If some or all questions can be answered in the affirmative, then the basis for making tentative generalizations exists. The problem then is to link these weakly based generalizations to a theory that has a broader evidential base. Initially, impressions are formed about "what goes with what." These observations are the basis for what is called inductive generalizing, or making very general conclusions from observing a limited number of instances of an event.

Phillip E. Converse's (1964) study of mass ideologies and elite ideologies has provided an example of inductive generalization. This study was designed to examine the extent to which different ideas about politics tend to go together for the same people. How these sets of relationships, or "structure," of ideas differed in the mass publics, as contrasted to the elite, or politically active publics, was the focus of Converse's study.

One set of conclusions in the study was based on responses to attitude questions that concerned matters of public policy. In general, these data indicated that mass publics and elite publics maintained belief systems that were very different. The nature of these differences was arrived at inductively by observing similarities and differences in attitudinal structures within and between mass and elite publics.

Correlation coefficients provided measures of the extent to which a favorable or unfavorable response to one attitude could be predicted from another attitude response by the individual. When views are systematically held so that one can predict a person's attitude on civil rights from his or her attitude on some other issue, such as welfare spending, we say that a high level of structure exists.

Converse looked at correlations between attitudes on eight foreign and domestic policy issues of an elite public (United States congressional candidates) and of the mass public (a cross section of the electorate) separately. He found a high degree of structure (that is, high correlations) among the eight policy issues for the elite public. In contrast, he found a low degree of structure (that is, low correlations) among the eight items for the mass public. In each instance, it was the *magnitude* of the correlations that led to the inference of the presence or absence of structure among attitudes. The fact that sizable correlations exist among all attitudes for elites suggested that structure existed for them; the fact that very meager if any correlations existed among the items for the mass public suggested the absence of structure for them. Finally, the large differences between the size of correlations for the two groups reaffirmed the difference in attitude structure between these mass and elite publics.

D. Refining explanations

Given the structure of an explanation, a major part of a scientist's effort lies in refining by conceptual analysis the explanation and the theory that underlies it. Three kinds of activities are involved: (1) Trying to formulate the assumptions, concepts, and conclusions of the explanation in a clearer and more explicit way; (2) trying to extend the coverage of the explanation by adding assumptions to the generalizations in the explanation that make it more comprehensive and precise (this includes trying to derive more testable statements from the existing theory and assumptions); and (3) trying to formulate plausible alternative explanations.

The Converse study of belief systems provided good examples of each of these activities. First, Converse discussed some of the diverse meanings of the term "ideology." One usage of the term included all possible ideas, while other uses included only some kinds of ideas about some kinds of things. Yet other uses of ideology included only "true" ideas. In any case, Converse decided to discuss "belief systems" rather than ideologies in his study to avoid ambiguity created by the diversity of uses that have been made of *ideology*. The concept "ideology" was too ambiguous to be useful because people have associated too many things with it.

Converse next specified that a belief system is a group of ideas that are functionally connected. By that he meant that one idea depends on another; or, if one idea is changed, then all other ideas will have to be changed by the person as well because the ideas depend on each other. The term *constraint* was defined to mean the extent to which a number of ideas in a belief system are functionally interdependent.

Converse's next step in the theorizing process was to specify many of the assumptions that were made. These assumptions took the form of a list of sources of idea constraints (or dependency of ideas on each other). Converse stated that some constraints are present because of logical relationships that are "seen" among ideas. Some kinds of connections between ideas are simply never made because these connections would be illogical.

Psychological sources of constraints between ideas were also listed. Converse noted that learning of relationships produces constraints because only certain relationships are learned within sets of experiences. Thus, some ideas go with other ideas. Social constraints are those that are produced by institutions or groups within the society. Churches, for example, teach a body of fairly coherent beliefs that often have social implications. Exposure to one church, therefore, would be expected to produce relationships between ideas different from exposure to some other church. And exposure would occur because of membership in a particular group, or residence at a particular location, or for some other social reason.

These assumptions lead one to conclude that many sources of constraint exist. Indeed, if all ideas were very important to the individual, then belief systems would be highly constrained. Converse assumed, on the basis of a fair amount of evidence, that personal importance of ideas varies considerably for different people. And importance of political policy is very low for mass publics.

The Converse study also provided an example of how the addition of assumptions (called "deductive elaboration") allows the development of a greater range of hypotheses than had existed before. Converse hypothesized that mass publics will have relatively low levels of ideological sophistication. Mass publics will not tend to think in terms of broad policy implications, such as "liberal or conservative" in order to comprehend the political world. When a sample of nonelite respondents was classified according to the extent to which broad conclusions are brought to bear on thinking about politics, this hypothesis was supported. Very few in the American public used broad conceptions, such as "liberal or conservative," to organize their thinking about policy issues.

Converse further hypothesized that low levels of constraint exist in mass publics because the majority of the population have low levels of political and ideological sophistication—because they do not use general dimensions like liberalism and conservatism by which to classify their ideas. This failure to use general ideas to classify issues is based on a lack of information about politics that the majority of United States citizens have.

Converse was able to reject some plausible alternative explanations for his findings about the bases of constraint by investigating the effects of education on the relationship between ideas. It is possible that ideological sophistication is merely a reflection of education and that degrees of constraint among ideas are due to educational levels rather than ideological sophistication. The fact that both ideological sophistication and constraint levels among ideas are related to education makes this plausible alternative view appear all the more likely. Converse checked the relationship between level of constraint and ideological sophistication within broad educational groupings of respondents in order to check the truth of this alternative explanation. He found that, regardless of education level, the relationship between ideological sophistication and constraint levels in thinking about policy issues was maintained. Thus, one plausible alternative explanation was rejected. (As we shall see later, there can be other explanations for generally high or generally low correlations, in addition to those mentioned here.)

E. Conceptual analysis

Clarification of assumptions, concepts, and conclusions usually involves a more explicit statement of what the assumptions are. Clarification also involves trying to clear up ambiguities concerning concepts and conclusions. In part, ambiguities stem from vagueness of the language employed by social scientists for definitions, and, in part, the ambiguities stem from the extent to which pressing value concerns are related to what is studied (the very relevance of social science to social life may act to cloud concerns of the scientist).

Analysis of verbal definitions and the logical structure of theories help to purge the logical blunders which seem to be so characteristic of theories and disciplines that contain fuzzy conceptualization. Explication in clear, explicit language so that every concept is carefully defined may also aid one to avoid mystification as well as certain commonsensical ambiguities that frequently appear. Indeed, one source of poor theorizing is the failure to articulate more completely the logical implications of assumptions that are contained in a theory. It is easy for logical implications to remain obscured when not explicitly noted. Again, this problem is, perhaps, most acute when work touches directly on highly valued aspects of life because it may be harder to analyze many aspects of problems relating to one's central values than it is to analyze other problems.

Another highly important purpose of conceptual analysis is to construct explanations of events that are plausible and that constitute alternative explanations to those we initially see as correct. Analysts ought not to be content with a single explanation of a phenomenon. They ought to invent several explanations that are plausible and that contain logically inconsistent generalizations. Creating plausible alternatives forces us out of mental ruts in theoretical creativity into which we all occasionally fall, requires us at least to consider unorthodox explanations which might not otherwise gain a hearing, and may provide that extra shove that our imaginations need to invent more adequate explanations.

F. Theoretical elaboration

In a theory, the addition of an assumption allows one to say more about the topic. More complete explanations result. In theories that concern several events, a limited number of additional assumptions help to generate large numbers of additional conclusions. A theory is made more comprehensive by adding assumptions which help to specify and clarify the conditions under which events are more or less likely to occur and processes that are involved in the event or the development of some state of affairs.

Adding relevant assumptions is usually called *elaboration* of the explanation or theory. The assumptions introduce new concepts that either are assumed to intervene in time between other concepts in the theory and what it is we want to explain or are assumed to come before other concepts which are assumed themselves to lead to what we wish to explain. The most important aspect of explanatory elaboration is that the new concepts have relevance for the conclusion of the explanation. It is sometimes easy to lose sight of the two central concerns of theory building—trying to explain an event in the most comprehensive and in the most precise way possible—once elaboration has been started.

One approach to elaborating theories is to look critically at the series of assumptions on which the theory is based. Are they logically consistent? Do they lead to hypotheses beyond those already explicit? Do they give rise to other generalizations that are inconsistent by implication? Diagramming the concepts and their interrelationship is often helpful in making implicit hypotheses explicit. Which concept leads to which concept?

For example, the idea of "time" is a very ambiguous notion in much social science theorizing. We define *cause* in terms of one concept systematically preceding another concept in a theoretically meaningful way. When this temporal relationship occurs, we say that the latter concept has been "caused" by the former concept. But in many cases it is nearly impossible to establish which variable precedes another variable. We assume, for example, that attitudes about partisan affiliation precede attitudes about specific policy issues, and that the former has some causal impact on the latter. (We see policies that members of our own party endorse, for instance, somewhat more favorably than we view policies that the opposition endorses.)

But how much confidence can we have in such assumptions? The precedence of partisan identification is based on two kinds of findings. First, surveys among young children suggest that attitudes about political parties appear sooner than attitudes about other things. Second, partisan identification is related to a greater number of attitudes and behaviors in statistically stronger ways than are other concepts. But we also know that partisan identification changes and that error appears in its measurement. Thus, it may be far from clear what the temporal relationships between partisan affiliation and other concepts are in particular instances. This problem is usually solved by simply imposing an explicit assumption of time ordering on the theory and data with which one is working.

Questions about ways to extend the explanation are also in order. What concepts and assumptions can be added to the explanation that are relevant and are likely to provide even more information about what we wish to explain? Can this particular explanation be logically linked to other explanations about similar phenomena? Can ideas from explanations of other phenomena be used to create novel explanations in the context of our problem?

New, tentative assumptions are introduced into the logical structure of the explanation. Attempts to derive new propositions are made; the extent to which new and theoretically interesting hypotheses can be derived from the tentative assumptions of the original explanation serves as one measure of the usefulness of the tentative assumption. If the tentative assumption has some value because it works in the above test, it is then incorporated into the explanation, and the process of questioning resumes. In any serious realm of inquiry, that process rarely stops for long.

It is also particularly valuable to raise questions about processes of behavior that may be involved in the occurrence of the events we study: Under what conditions is the explanation likely to be true or not true? Why is that? What are the conditions that increase the accuracy of prediction of the theory? Decrease the accuracy of prediction? What specific social and/or psychological processes are involved? What kinds of indirect relationships are involved? (By indirect relationships we mean those relationships that involve more than two concepts in which concept A is not related to concept C in a direct way, but is related to concept B which *is* related to concept C.)

Thus, theorizing concerns applying logical analysis to assumptions that one has made in order to explain a phenomenon. Concepts and assumptions are made explicit in the process. But most important of all, a type of scientific imagination is central to combining assumptions, observations, and conclusions to form an explanation. And once formed, the explanation is further refined by a questioning process that is based on the analyst's creative imagination.

Theorizing involves imaginative speculation, but the speculation must eventually confront tests of empirical reality. The constraint of making ideas correspond to reality is the most difficult and challenging of all. Even if everyone is persuaded of the theory's plausibility, the data may not be. Scientists must try to invent explanations that explain an increasingly large proportion of the behavior they are trying to understand.

G. Retroduction

retroduction

In the process of determining explanations for observed events, social scientists often reason *from* conclusions to reasons *for* conclusions. We call this inference process *retroduction*, in contrast with deduction and induction. In retroduction, we try to think of plausible reasons why some event could have occurred in an attempt to construct an explanation of why the event did occur.

In everyday life, people sometimes reach conclusions and make up reasons for them later. In the absence of other information, these reasons appear plausible. Similarly, social scientists think up plausible reasons which are accepted only provisionally until systematic testing is conducted.

An example of retroductive reasoning appears in a study of the decline of trust in the national government during the last decade (Miller, 1972). Miller first tried to explain the decrease in trust by reasoning that distrust might have been caused by opposition to public policy. Perhaps distrust has increased because opposition to government policy in respect to civil rights or the Vietnam war had increased during the 1960s.

However, Miller found some results which did not fit this explanation. Civil rights *supporters* declined in trust of the government more than did civil rights opponents, even though the battle for legal integration had essentially been won during the time. Why might that be? How are we to reconcile these findings with our previous ideas?

Looking more closely at his data to solve this puzzle, Miller turned up a possible clue. In 1966 (after passage of the Civil Rights acts of 1964 and 1965), political trust rose among Blacks and fell among whites. After that, trust among Blacks plummeted so drastically and steadily that it equalled the falling trust of whites by 1968 and had fallen well below it by 1970.

Perhaps the passage of these laws raised hopes among Blacks and raised fear, insecurity, or resentment among whites. Later, public policy failed to wipe out racial discrimination, and "Trust in the government may have thus declined sharply among Blacks after 1966 because of frustration arising out of unfulfilled expectations" (Miller, 1972, p. 13).

At this point, Miller completed the new explanation of the surprising finding. The act of retroduction—going from the unexpected finding to a new hypothesis—is done. Blacks became more cynical because civil rights legislation raised hopes higher than it delivered. The new generalization adds the concept of "unfulfilled expectations" to the concept of "opposition to governmental policy" (which still seems to help explain distrust among white segregationists). This combination sounds plausible, especially since something like it has been said many times by many authorities to account for similar phenomena. Our minds might come to rest comfortably here. But Miller's did not. For, it is one thing to invent a satisfactory explanation which fits the evidence, and another to test it. *Inventing an explanation does not make it valid.*

First, Miller deduced some implications from the new hypothesis. If "unfulfilled expectations" are the source of growth in political distrust, then:

1. A higher percentage of Blacks in 1970 than in 1964 should feel that the Civil Rights movement is going too slowly.
2. Distrust should have increased more among impatient Blacks than among other Blacks.
3. Similarly, political distrust should have increased more among whites who are impatient with the progress of the Civil Rights movement than among whites who think it is moving too fast.
4. Distrust should be increasing least among whites who are satisfied with civil rights progress.

(All of these deductions assume that impatience with the progress of civil rights might indicate "unfulfilled expectations.") All four implications were upheld by the data.

But Miller sought much stronger evidence. After all, this finding is based on responses to a single question. Other questions might yield other answers. Also, other issues, such as Vietnam, might not affect political trust through unfulfilled expectations. And Miller created further challenges to his hypothesis by retroducing additional explanations of the same data, such as: (1) distrust results when people see no differences between the policy alternatives offered by the major political parties or their leaders; and (2) distrust results from dissatisfaction with expected or perceived policy performance of the party in power.

After eliminating all of these rival hypotheses through extensive data analysis, Miller introduced measures of discrepancy between the respondent's policy preferences and the respondent's perception of the policies

proffered by the parties. He found that these measures of policy dissatisfaction accounted for substantial variation in political trust, even when
all the other variables were considered as well. In other words, declining
political trust was associated with "unfulfilled expectations." So, what
started as a surprising observation ends up explained by a well-tested new
generalization.

This example has many instructive features. First, there is the problem:
Why do some people trust the government while others do not? Second,
there is the persistent attempt to find something common to all of the
trusting people to distinguish them from the distrusting in some way that
would explain their different attitude toward the government. This is an
attempt to abstract (select) one relevant facet from many existing facets
and then generalize that facet from some cases to all cases. Miller sought
a new concept "to unite phenomena which without [the concept] are either
surprising, anomalous, or wholly unnoticed" (Hanson, 1958, p. 121). He
sought, in short, to *create*, by seeing, as others have not, the *relevance* of
some facets of the situation to each other. This seeing as others have not
is the creative essence of science.

Finally, there is the empirical test: Miller's first hypothesis seemed right,
but he still checked it out on further data. Empirical testing is what distin-
guishes scientific retroduction from ordinary rationalization. Instead of
resting comfortably with their new reasons, scientists challenge them with
new facts. It is crucial that the facts be new ones, and not the very ones
which suggested the new hypothesis. For, since the new hypothesis was
tailored by Miller to fit the original facts, new facts are needed to challenge
the hypothesis.

The scientist who makes the challenge may not be the one who makes
the discovery, but the rules of science, unlike those of polite conversation,
demand that the challenge be made.

What is perhaps most surprising to some people is the almost accidental
nature of retroduction. For those who expect scientists to predict everything
successfully from deductive theorizing this is quite disillusioning. Deduction, we recall, merely brings out what is already contained in the premises.
For all of successful scientific inquiry to be deductive, scientists must begin
with premises which unerringly embody all possible knowledge. But scientists are human, so why should they have omniscient powers of deduction
which are denied to the rest of humanity?

Retroduction is also disappointing to those who see science as merely
"luck" which becomes institutionalized and enforced doctrine. For, it is the
creative imagination, disciplined mind, and careful accumulation of knowledge which permit the scientist to go from the mechanical discarding of
hypotheses that do not work to the identification of those that do work. And
it is the norms of empiricism which stop retroduced hypotheses from
becoming self-perpetuating, self-serving half-truths.

Retroduction is also surprising to those who think that scientists simply collect observations and then summarize those observations in generalizations. This view that science stops with induction is false and misleading, for several reasons (Hempel, 1966). First, if all we have is a summary of the observations, then no new concepts can occur in generalizations; consequently, scientific discovery would be impossible. Miller could never go from a concept of "opposition to government policy" to one of "unfulfilled expectations."

Second, if science merely gathers "all the facts" without prior selection, then it could never get going, for there are an infinite number and variety of facts in the world (Hempel, 1966). Miller started with the hypothesis that political distrust results from opposition to government policies. Without such a hypothesis, there could have been no test of "relevance" for data. He would still be "collecting all the facts," such as the respondents' height, weight, eye color, hair color, nose length . . . ad infinitum. Thus, science is not and cannot be based on pure induction.

Much has been written about the rules and procedures of science. Some textbooks have even developed lists of such rules and procedures, calling the result "science." But these lists are no more all there is to science than clothes are all there is to the person. Science is the ceaseless quest for making things "explicable as a matter of course"—the "struggle for intelligibility" (Hanson, 1958, p. 87). Retroduction is no bastard of science, but its progenitor. We fit data into patterns retroductively; we elaborate the patterns deductively and test them inductively, but the propositions that endure are usually retroduced, not deduced or induced. The scientist shuttles back and forth between data and theory. How else could it be?

III. TESTING HYPOTHESES

Once explanations are clearly and explicitly formulated, we wish to find out just how adequate these explanations are. For, no matter how elegant the logical structure of an explanation may be and no matter how complex and numerous the assumptions in the theory that generates the explanation, we want theories that work. The ultimate test of a social science explanation, clearly then, is how well it allows us to predict the way the world is. Prediction involves ascertaining the extent to which observations of behavior agree with what the theory specifies the case should be. The test of the adequacy of a theory then is the answer to the question: How well does the world correspond to the way the theory states the world should look?

One begins the testing procedures by setting up what is called a "model." This model involves an explicit, hypothetical deductive structure. Each assumption along with definitions of the concepts that appear in the assumptions is explicitly listed in this hypothetical deductive structure, even when done "after the fact" as in retroduction. Hypotheses that logically follow from the assumptions and that we wish to test are also explicitly stated. Finally, logic that links assumptions to hypotheses is also explicitly stated.

As an example of this, we will use a study of voting decisions. Converse (1962) examined the way that people use information in deciding either to support their party's presidential candidate or to defect from their party's nominee. An early step in the inquiry was to set up a model, based on prior investigations, about how the relationship of information and voting behavior should look.

Citing other studies, Converse argued that voting decisions are influenced by both longer-term and shorter-term forces. The long-term forces he identified as concepts that are associated with more than the election at hand, such as partisan self-identification, which is viewed as a moderately permanent influence on political behavior. Short-term forces are concepts associated with the pending election and only with this election, such as perceptions of the particular candidates who happen to be running.

Converse defined "stability" as voting for the candidate of one's own party, while "defection" involved voting for the opposition party's candidate. It was assumed for purposes of the study that defection arises from short-term forces. One of these forces might be information available about the candidates and issues in the campaign. However, it is well-known that people tend to perceive, retain, and recall information selectively to support their own long-standing loyalties. These loyalties become stronger as people become more and more involved in politics.

Thus, Converse's initial theoretical model concluded that people who are more exposed to short-term forces away from their own party and toward the other party will be more likely to defect in their voting. It was further, and more concretely, expected that people who are more politically involved and who have more information will defect less than those who are less politically involved and who have less information. These assumptions and conclusions comprised Converse's initial model, a model that was subjected to considerable questioning in the remainder of his study.

It is, of course, the hypotheses that are tested directly in the research. The assumptions (the theory) that lead to the hypotheses gather support indirectly as more and more hypotheses that are derived from the initial assumptions are supported by empirical evidence. In his study of information flow, Converse began by hypothesizing that defection from one's own party would be less among those who were politically involved and consequently were in the flow of political information and had large stores of information about politics. These specific hypotheses followed from Converse's theory of voting behavior and were formulated in the specific terms of his study.

Theories are more general in content than hypotheses and also involve a larger number of assumptions than analysts can cope with in any single study. Thus, evidence that supports a particular hypothesis provides some reason to believe that the theory from which the hypothesis was derived is true. This evidence is rarely conclusive because there are always a large number of plausible alternative theories from which the hypothesis could have been derived. One may be right for the wrong reasons. Occasionally it will, however, be possible to provide evidence that could not possibly exist if a given theory were true. One strategy of theorizing is to try to formulate and eliminate as many of these plausible alternative hypotheses as possible.

For example, in the Converse study of information flow, the theory relates to the general impact of long- and short-term forces on partisan voting behavior. People vote in accord with long-term forces unless these forces are disrupted by opposing short-term forces. This is an extremely general set of assumptions that extends far beyond ideas of voting stability and voting defection.

Evidence, however, that bears on notions of defection also relates to the more general theory. If the more involved and informed in fact defect less than others, then some further support (but not conclusive proof) is given to the original theoretical position. If the more involved and informed defect more than others, then the hypothesis is challenged seriously and some question may be appropriately raised about the adequacy of the theory.

It is possible that an alternative explanation may better account for observations. Converse, for example, in testing the hypothesis that the more politically involved defect less than the less involved, found that the least politically involved were less likely than the most involved to defect in the 1958 congressional election. These findings suggested an alternative explanation: Defection depends on the flow of information. Those who are less involved but who are also exposed to political information are *very likely* to defect, while those who are less involved and not exposed to political information are *very unlikely* to defect. Thus, the effect of involvement on defection is different, depending on the extent of exposure to information, reflecting the concept of interaction.

In further testing this alternative explanation on voters in general elections during the 1950s, Converse found support for the revised hypothesis that one's susceptibility to defection depends on the amount of information that one has available. This finding suggests, incidentally, that wise campaign managers would do well to orient their media campaigns to the politically uninvolved potential voters, for those are the most easily won. The findings from this study are alternatives in the sense that they provide a more fully elaborated view of behavior. They do not necessarily provide a view that contradicts the initial theoretical position.

The assumptions of a theory must also be subject to increasing skepticism to the extent that hypotheses derived from the theory are not supported by evidence when put to a test. Two points are important: (1) The test that confronts our theoretically generated hypotheses is based on evidence that is external to the theorist. As such, this evidence is less subject to involuntary perceptual and cognitive distortion. The evidence is also public. And (2) it is the test and the test alone that generates criteria by which we know how much confidence we ought to place in the hypotheses and in the more general theory from which the hypotheses are derived.

Like it or not, data collected by opinion surveys and other scientific techniques are beyond the control of the investigator. If people who are exposed to media defect more than others, then this is the way the world is; and the fact is external to the investigator. The same findings would, presumably, be replicated by other social scientists who used the same procedures on the same sample. No amount of reflection or selective perception changes these facts.

While interpretations *are* subject to the creativity of the analyst, it is the finding that the more involved are more likely to be susceptible to defection under conditions of high exposure that leads us to question our initial hypothesis. No matter how elegant our theoretical framework may be, the proof of the scientific pudding is in the eating. And a later study by Dreyer (1971) conducted on data collected in the 1960s *did* question Converse's findings.

A. Measurement theory

In deciding how to test hypotheses, a measurement theory must be established. A *measurement theory* is a set of assumptions about the way the world of theory is related to the world of observations. Some kind of measurement theory, an empirical theory of the same kind as any other scientific theory about behavior, is always assumed (implicitly if not explicitly) whenever scientific concepts, hypotheses, and theories are discussed. A diagram (adapted from Torgerson, 1958, p. 5) should help to clarify the role of a measurement theory. The Converse study of information flow will serve as an example.

Figure 2.2 provides a pictorial representation of a theory, concepts, hypothesis, and measures or indicators for the concepts in the hypothesis. The Cs (C_1, C_2, C_3, C_4, and C_5) are concepts. C_1, C_2, and C_3 are included in the theory. These stand for the ideas of long- and short-term forces and partisan vote choice, respectively. These are the concepts that led to Converse's initial hypothesis that political involvement decreases defection in voting.

The concepts in the hypothesis, exposure to information and vote defection, are represented by C_4 and C_5, respectively, in the diagram. Lines that are drawn between each of the concepts indicate a logical (theoretical) relationship between the concepts that are linked. This relationship may suggest that one concept "causes" another, or that a relationship occurs with several concepts in the theory. Note that the relationships among concepts in the theory, C_1 to C_3, are taken as true until evidence suggests

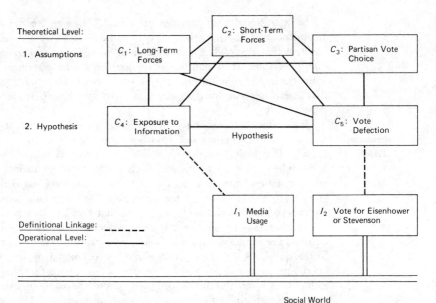

Theoretical Level:

1. Assumptions

2. Hypothesis

Definitional Linkage:
Operational Level:

Social World

FIGURE 2.2   Relationships between conceptual and operational levels in theory building.

otherwise and are used to derive the hypothesis, the relationship between C_4 and C_5. It is this hypothesis and not the theoretical relationship that is directly tested.

A definitional linkage, portrayed by the broken lines in Figure 2.2, specifies the empirical meaning of C_4 as media usage and C_5 as vote defection. In the Converse study, for example, use of the media was measured by the extent to which respondents say that they received information about the campaign from each medium—television, radio, newspapers, and magazines. Vote defection was measured by whether respondents reported voting for the candidate of the other party (that is, self-identified Democrats reporting an Eisenhower vote, and self-identified Republicans reporting a Stevenson vote).

Converse was using one specific set of questions to measure media usage. A variety of other questions, such as "Did you watch any news about the election on TV last night?" could have been used instead. It is also important to note that many different *kinds* of indicators could have been used. These would involve very different ways of getting information about respondents' usage of media. For example, usage could have been measured by the number of subscriptions to news magazines and newspapers, ownership of TV sets (a poor measure since almost all people report owning at least one), or by diaries about radio, TV, newspaper, and news magazine usage. This topic will be considered further in the chapters on validity (Chapter 6) and indirect methods of measurement (Chapter 10).

The operational level provides the actual indicators for the concepts that are included in the hypothesis. These indicators, as we saw above, are the answers that respondents in a national survey gave when asked *specific questions* about their political party loyalty, media exposure, and vote. It is the pattern of relationships among responses to these particular questions that comprises empirical *evidence* against the initial hypothesis of Converse's study.

operational   Measurement theory concerns the linkage between concepts and indica-
definitions   tors in a study. Operational definitions are always based on measurement theories that assign empirical meaning to concepts. Whenever we wish to know whether or not a concept, such as C_4, exposure to information, is a characteristic of a person or a group of persons, we first define what the empirical characteristics of the concept C_4 are. We say here that people are exposed to information to the extent that they use the media.

The operational definition stipulates which *specific indicators* (or *observations*) are to be assigned which specific meanings. These are the responses to the questions: "Did you read about the campaign in any newspapers?" "Did you listen to any speeches or discussions about the campaign on the radio?" "Did you watch any programs about the campaign on television?" "Did you read about the campaign in any magazines?" The number of yes responses to each of these questions was then tallied, and a large number of positive answers was assumed to indicate a high level of media exposure on the respondent's part while a low number of positive answers was assumed to indicate a low level of media exposure. Similarly, high exposure to these media was assumed to define a respondent's being located in the midst of a great deal of information and subject to a great flow of information. Low exposure was taken as an indicator that a respondent was not bombarded by a great deal of political information. Note that one concept may be represented by one of several indicators among many alternative possibilities.

One never asks whether operational definitions are "true" or "false." But several evaluative criteria must be brought to bear on definitions. Definitions ought to: (1) assign empirical and logical meaning to concepts in an explicit and precise way; and (2) assign meaning to concepts so that indicators of the concepts relate to indicators of other concepts in ways that are predicted by theory. In other words, definitions ought to be unambiguous and clear in what they refer to, and definitions ought to be constructed so that the concepts fit into theories. If concepts are defined so that they fit into theories, then we can be assured that our definitions are useful. Beyond this, criteria for definitions become less clear, although some definitions may be more useful in theories than other definitions, just as some definitions may lead to measures that are accurate and precise more easily than other measures.

All scientific definitions include assumptions that link properties of events to concepts in direct ways. These assumptions about the way that properties of events represent concepts comprise the measurement theory to which we referred above. Operationalization of concepts must clearly involve fairly explicit measurement theories. Operationalization includes carrying out specified procedures and then evaluating the results in order to ascertain the presence or absence of a concept. The business of selecting operations for concepts must include the search for evidence of the congruence between the operation and the concept. Operationalizations, therefore, must contain a statement of all the plausible outcomes of the procedure. The relationship between procedures and outcomes is, itself, a hypothesis that is assumed to be true and is based on yet additional assumptions. All are included in the measurement theory.

In the Converse study of information flow, for example, the operational measure of exposure to information was to ask each respondent to assess his or her own exposure to the campaign in regard to each of four media, and then to classify each respondent in terms of the number of media to which he or she reported exposure. The operation includes the interviewer asking the questions in the interviewing situation in a carefully prescribed way. The outcome of the procedure is the set of responses to the questions and the summation of the responses in a straightforward numerical way.

A variety of assumptions are involved in the above example of an operational measure. It is assumed that the respondent is telling the truth. It is assumed that neither the interviewer nor the respondent has behaved in ways that would distort responses to the question. It is assumed that responses to the question are in fact related to what we conceptualize as the "real" meaning of exposure to information. It is assumed that the classifications that we assign to the different possible responses represent the "actual" relationships between the responses and that these classifications are related to other classifications in the ways that are assumed by the theory. It is assumed that each medium "counts the same" for the exposure index. Finally, it is assumed that errors are distributed among both respondents and responses so that no systematic bias in reporting media behavior exists, that is, that the errors in different directions cancel each other out. (In most studies, this involves assumptions of randomness in error.)

We also assume that a person who is exposed to information has been exposed through the media in question, and not through other media such as personal contacts. Of course, this assumption is mostly false, for surely one gets some information from friends. The error of this particular assumption illustrates the importance of making such assumptions explicit, so that they can be challenged, as this one might be.

Measurement theory is involved in justifying the scientific operations and in classifying characteristics of individuals according to results. The major significance of a measurement theory, however, is in the assumptions that are made when concepts are used. The measurement theory is based on specific assumptions concerning what indicators reflect what properties that the concepts specify in which ways.

"Validity" is concerned with the adequacy of a measurement theory and its specific measurements. "Are we measuring what we think that we are measuring?" is but another way of inquiring into the relationship between concepts and measures. The more adequate the measurement theory, the more valid the specific measures. Social scientists need to become more aware of the assumptions that they make in measurement, and consequently, scientists need to deal with measurement theories explicitly.

One example of what would appear to be a very clearly defined variable, arrest record, appears on analysis to be quite ambiguous. Fogelson and Hill (1968) noted that having been arrested is not necessarily an indicator of criminal propensities in the Black community in Detroit. First, although arrests are recorded, these records are not modified once one is tried and acquitted or released without trial. As far as the statistics are concerned, an arrest is just that, regardless of guilt or innocence. Second, a very large proportion of young adult Black males are arrested in the Detroit ghetto because the relatively high crime rates in the vicinity are associated with increased consequent police activity. Together, these facts grossly modify our notion of what an arrest record really means.

It is vital to note that all assumptions in the measurement theory, such as the assumption of validity in the study mentioned above, must be true if we are going to be able to interpret the test of our hypotheses as we intend. The possibility that one or more of the assumptions that are specified in the measurement theory are incorrect always suggests at least one plausible alternative explanation to that provided by our theory. This is one of the reasons that scientific investigation is so largely dedicated to analysis of the assumptions and measures that are used.

B. Units of analysis

Every scientific investigation establishes a set of cases or units for analysis. The way in which a specific set of cases is selected governs the generalizability of the conclusions one may draw from a study. Procedures consist of sampling from a larger set of cases or randomly selecting individuals from a prespecified universe.

Results of specific analyses can only be generalized to larger populations if the sampling procedures are adequate so that the results can be taken as estimates of the results that would have been attained had the larger population been studied rather than just a sample from the larger population. Sampling involves a set of rules (or procedures) that governs selecting a relatively small number of cases to represent a larger number of cases. Generalizability of results depends on how observations are selected for inclusion in a study. A few examples of sampling problems follow.

Sampling by randomly *assigning* individuals to test groups provides some assurance that some kinds of bias are probably not being introduced into experimental research. Random *selection* of respondents in nonexperimental research performs a function that is similar to random assignment in experimental research in this regard. An unknown and most likely large number of events beyond those included in a study probably affect the events included in the study. Randomization and random selection function to control the impact of these other variables. Plausible alternative explanations should always include the possibility that a given sample is biased in that, prior to the study, the various groups being compared are not equivalent.

Converse's studies were based on samples of the United States electorate during the 1950s. The samples were designed to represent the electorate at that time, and no contrary evidence has been cited to discount this assumption. Dreyer (1971), however, challenged whether Converse's findings concerning the relationship between involvement and defection could be generalized and extended to the 1960s. Dreyer hypothesized that the 1950s were unusually calm and tranquil, while in the 1960s social conflict and change were everywhere, and TV exposure had increased greatly. Conflict instigated interest in much larger proportions of the electorate, and this change fundamentally altered the relationship between vote defection, political involvement, and exposure to the media. The time periods, not the sample, are responsible for the inability to generalize conclusions in this instance.

Yet another problem in the testing process is the assessment of evidence in specific tests. Just what kinds of evidence "count for" a hypothesis, and what kinds of evidence "count against" a hypothesis? Although the complete answers to these questions are tied to all of the things that we have been discussing, some additional comments ought to be made.

A well-elaborated measurement theory specifies which indicators measure which particular concepts. The particular categories used in the measurement process also need to be specified. We must specify what specific configurations of indicators support or lead our hypothesis to be questioned. We also wish to reduce the number of ambiguous relationships that are possible for a given test. Ideally, all possible configurations of indicators would be sorted into those that support the hypothesis being tested and those that draw the hypothesis into question in a theoretically meaningful way.

In the case of Converse's study of information flow, for example, the hypothesis that defection decreased as exposure to information increased was supported if and only if heavier media users among respondents defected at lower rates than lighter media users among respondents. It is assumed that, for the hypothesis to be supported, moderate media users should defect less than light users but more than heavy users.

Of course, this supportive configuration was *not* found in the Converse study. Groups of both high and low media users were much more susceptible to defection than were more moderate users of the media.

C. Elaboration of relationships

Elaboration of relationships among variables is one way that theories can be extended. Once theoretically justified and explicit hypotheses have been established, additional variables can be introduced. These have several purposes: to specify further conditions under which particular relationships may occur, to make predictions more accurate, to specify the presence or absence of processes, and to test a variety of other hypotheses that make the theory more complete in explanation and accurate in prediction.

independent variable dependent variable   In elaborating relationships, we utilize the terms "independent variable" and "dependent variable." Some variables precede other variables in hypotheses and theories. The dependent variable is the variable we are most interested in. It is dependent on other variables that precede it in a theoretical sense for the characteristics it assumes. The likelihood of defection, for instance in the Converse study, depends on the degree of exposure to media that characterizes respondents. Media exposure is hypothesized to affect defection.

Variables that do not depend on other variables, or variables that come first in a temporal sense in hypotheses are called independent, or "antecedent," variables. In "causal" hypotheses, these variables are causes, while the dependent variables are the effects. Exposure to media is an example of an independent variable, in the above study.

intervening variables   Variables that come between dependent and independent variables are called "intervening variables." They intervene between two other variables. In the case of the Converse information flow study, exposure to mass media was assumed to intervene between political involvement and voting defection, because exposure tended to disrupt a relationship that would otherwise have existed, and personal political involvement was assumed to be an individual characteristic of long standing.

Various strategies for dealing with independent, dependent, and intervening variables are involved in elaboration. Most generally, one starts with a simple hypothesis about two variables, such as the hypothesis that relatively high degrees of political involvement lead to decreased rates of defection. Intervening variables that are theoretically related to both the independent and dependent variables may then be introduced into the hypothesis. Converse suggested that additional information, as measured by the extent of media exposure, might disrupt or intensify the original relationship between involvement and defection.

He in fact discovered that the relationship between political involvement and defection varied with amount of exposure. Those who were moderately exposed to mass media had greater rates of defection than those with either lesser or greater amounts of exposure. The moderately exposed, Converse argued, were sufficiently involved to expose themselves to possibly conflicting information, but not so involved that selectivity processes forced all incoming information into preexisting and consistent molds. It was possible therefore to defect.

The Dreyer critique of the Converse study showed yet another type of analysis that is used in elaborating relationships. Dreyer explained the discrepancies between his findings and Converse's findings by referring to **antecedent** the social and political context of the studies. The context is an "antecedent" **variable** variable since it can be conceptualized as encompassing all of the other variables within a theoretical context.

Dreyer argued that as the tranquil and apolitical 1950s gave way to the turbulent and politicized 1960s, a much greater amount of political information was developed and communicated. At the same time, a much larger group of people became deeply involved in politics. Finally, with the advent of saturation television, large proportions of the population could be regularly exposed to pictorial journalism. These social and political changes resulted in different groups of people being exposed to media. This, in turn, resulted in people who were least involved in politics defecting to a greater extent than the moderately or highly politically involved. Thus, the variable, "situational context," is used to explain the differences in findings between the two studies.

A large number of different kinds of theoretical implications can be tested in the process of elaboration by using intervening and antecedent variables that are initially hypothesized to suppress, maintain, or enlarge the original relationship. One of the best sources of ideas about this process was Rosenberg's (1968) notion of analysis in "pursuit of an idea." Variables were introduced to make sure that the findings are not explained away by some other relationships.

Yet more antecedent and intervening variables were introduced to specify the kinds of conditions under which the original relationship was least and most likely to occur, and the kinds of processes that were involved in the operation of the original relationship. Rosenberg observed the *way* that the original relationship changed *within* classifications of an additional (antecedent or intervening) variable in order to theorize inductively about and test a vast array of different aspects of the original relationship.

All of the considerations that have been mentioned in this section are relevant in the process of elaboration. A theoretical structure that includes explicit note of assumptions, hypotheses, and concepts is established; a measurement theory about which indicators measure what and how is specified; and consideration is given to sampling, assessment of evidence, and to both validity and generalizability.

D. Replications and extensions

Replications provide new opportunities for social scientists' hypotheses to be challenged. Conducted under conditions that repeat those of the original study, replication tests the consistency of findings. By altering the conditions, extensions of the study can determine the robustness of specific hypotheses under these slightly altered conditions. Replication may be conducted in two ways: by conducting and analyzing new studies that repeat all the basic features of the original one, and by observing what happens to the original relationship among subgroups of the original set of observations.

New studies that scrutinize the results that prior analysts have reported comprise the normal idea of *extension* or *modified replication*. The challenge that such studies involve is one of the things that makes science a marketplace of ideas. When extensions are conducted, the procedures used in the original study are also brought under scrutiny. Dreyer's extension of the Converse study provided an example of how valuable this process can be for gaining additional understanding of social processes.

A second kind of extension involves the use of control variables. Respondents are divided into groups according to categories of some third variable that is assumed to be *unrelated* to the variables included in the original hypothesis. Tests are then conducted to ascertain whether the original hypothesis is supported with *each* group or not. The question here, of course, is whether variables that should have *no* influence on the original relationship do or do not affect it in some way. This test is important because a variety of kinds of error can be isolated in this manner.

Testing and, in particular, extension and replication, lead to modification of theories. The studies of the effects of information flow on voting defection comprise but one example of modification due to further questioning of prior results. Although specific theories cannot be verified or falsified in any ultimate sense, researchers are led to alter theories when evidence is adduced against them. The resistance that we sometimes show in failing to reject or modify incorrect theories doubtlessly varies from one social scientist to another.

Nonetheless, modifications in theories and perspectives do occur. When new views emerge, it is important to test them. It is also important to continue to test rather well-accepted views under new and differing conditions. If questions are never raised, then possible false views are never challenged. It is a hallmark of science that no views remain immune to challenge.

IV. VERIFICATION AND FALSIFICATION

There is much misunderstanding about the degree of finality that results from testing hypotheses. A theory is neither verified nor falsified by empirical testing. Nor are hypotheses verified or falsified in a final or definitive way by empirical testing.

Theories are neither verified nor falsified by testing because they are not directly tested; hypotheses are what is directly tested. Theories are tested only indirectly through rather specific hypotheses derived by innovative social scientists from the theories. Thus, all the hypotheses that an investigator derives from a theory may be rejected when tested, but the theory may still be true. Or, all the hypotheses that an investigator derives may be supported when tested, but the theory may still be false. This degree of uncertainty is not normally assumed but certainly is possible.

Hypotheses may be supported or rejected for the wrong reasons as well. True hypotheses may be rejected or false hypotheses accepted, because of the probabilistic way hypotheses are tested. For a single study, probability theory tells us the likelihood of whether these kinds of mistakes will occur, but that probability of error in inference is never zero or one in normal testing procedures. The purpose in exact replication of a study is to determine if one of these rare events occurred in the original study.

Neither hypotheses nor theories can be verified in an ultimate sense, moreover, because of what we may call the "inductive character of science" (Hempel, 1966). It is necessary to assume that events occur in a regular and patterned way, and that we can find out what these patterns are in order to speak meaningfully of a science in the first place. But specific patterns and regularities in behavior may be altered as new events occur or as other events intervene. Just because the sun has always come up, for example, does not guarantee that the sun always will come up; the sun's prior behavior just makes it appear very likely, but not certain, that the sun will rise tomorrow. It is always possible, if improbable, that the sun will explode in the near future or that other factors might prevent the sun from coming up tomorrow. Indeed, the probability that any future event will occur can never be zero or one, even though these limits are reached in our minds. We will simply have to wait until tomorrow to discover the answer to this question with certainty.

Theories and hypotheses are never falsified in a final way because of the ever-present existence of plausible alternative explanations for why evidence failed to support a given hypothesis. Rosenberg (1968), for example, discussed the possibility of "spurious non-correlations," that is, the absence of the appearance of a relationship between variables *because* an additional variable that has not been controlled is suppressing the relationship. Once the variable is controlled, the true relationship emerges. Error in observation, for example, can never be eliminated. In most tests, it is always possible to introduce additional variables that will account for rejection of a hypothesis under test conditions. We can always "explain away" findings that do not support our hypotheses in a strict logical sense.

Thus, theories and hypotheses can never be *ultimately* verified on logical grounds, and they can never be *ultimately* falsified on more practical operational grounds. Theories and hypotheses, however, certainly can and are made more or less plausible, and the most plausible theory is the one for which we have the strongest evidential support. And it is this theory that is to be provisionally "believed" or "accepted" until another theory gains superior evidential support. Scientific knowledge is knowledge under conditions of uncertainty. Other arenas of human experience should be investigated by those who desire knowledge with absolute certainty.

V. SUMMARY

The scientific method often has as its purposes the testing of hypotheses generated from theory. The process of testing derives conclusions based upon the evidence that has supported or failed to support the hypothesis. These conclusions may be considered inferences. The logic of analysis is concerned with the relationship between these inferences, or conclusions, and the evidence available for supporting them. One type of logic is oriented toward the deductive validity, or whether premises lead to a conclusion; this aspect is relevant when we reason from theories to hypotheses. The second type, inductive validity, requires more than valid premises for the conclusion to be considered valid. Scientific explanations need to be concerned with inductive validity because they are generalizations about some recurrent feature of behavior.

In the scientific approach to explanation of phenomena, a third process beyond deduction and induction is used. Retroduction refers to the use of conclusions in generating possible reasons for those conclusions. These explanations then serve as a hypothesis-generating activity, in and of themselves. Therefore alternative rival explanations for a conclusion are tested so it can be determined whether they may be discarded.

A measurement theory specifies how the theory is related to observations. In testing theory, operational definitions of the concepts must be developed which relate the theoretical aspects to observable, measurable aspects of behavior. Thus, the operational level provides the actual measures of the concepts that are included in the hypothesis.

chapter **3**

SELECTION
AND FORMULATION
OF A RESEARCH PROBLEM

I. SELECTING A TOPIC FOR RESEARCH

The range of potential topics for social research is as broad as the range of social behavior itself. The range of topics that have actually been selected for inquiry is, of course, much narrower. Yet even in one research area—for example, in the relations among groups of different ethnic or religious background—investigations have covered a vast field, including studies of how such groups act toward one another and feel and think about one another; how they differ in their traditions, beliefs, personalities, culture, and the way they treat their children; how they grow to be what they are; how they respond to attempts at changing their relationship to another group; and so on. These inquiries have been conducted in many parts of the world; they have involved members of many ethnic and religious groups in many walks of life.

The selection of the topic may arise from a concern with some social problem (for example, unemployment, the population explosion, urban problems, alienation, pollution, international conflict), or from an interest in some general theme or area of behavior (for example, aggression, achievement motivation, attitude change, voting), or from some body of theory (psychoanalytic theory, theories about the nature of learning, theories about the consistency of attitudes and social relations, role theory, and so on). Actually, there is no sharp distinction between topics arising from these various sources; often the same general topic can be approached either with an emphasis on contributing to the solution of a social problem or with an emphasis on contributing to theoretical knowledge; frequently there is a combination of both kinds of interest.

For example, research on relationships among ethnic groups may be approached on the basis of a concern with reducing prejudice and discrimination; or from a more abstract interest in attitudes, their development, structure, function, change, and/or relation to overt behavior; or with a combination of practical and theoretical interests. By way of illustration of

50

each approach, let us consider three programs of research in this area: one that focused on the effects of personal contact, of which an interracial housing study (Deutsch and Collins, 1951) was a part; another that concerned the personality structure of prejudiced individuals, reported in *The Authoritarian Personality* (Adorno, *et al.*, 1950); and a third that investigated the effectiveness of different approaches to changing attitudes in relation to the function the particular attitude serves for the particular individual (Katz, 1942; Katz, Sarnoff, and McClintock, 1956; and other publications).

The research group from which the interracial housing study developed was set up in the middle 1940s; its explicit concern was with the social problem of prejudice and discrimination against minority racial and religious groups. The group decided to study the effects of personal contact with members of a disliked group not on the basis of any clear theoretical foundation but because research and experience in the field of intergroup relations suggested that such contact might be a potent influence in the reduction of prejudice. The study focused on occupancy patterns largely because the "experience survey" (see Chapter 4) found that many housing experts considered this a crucial variable. In other words, the problem, the setting, and the major variable to be studied were selected because they were believed to be relevant to the social problems of prejudice and discrimination. However, in planning the study, the investigators asked themselves *why* different occupancy patterns might lead to differences in racial attitudes; that is, what the underlying dynamics of attitude change under these conditions might be: a theoretical question. It seemed to them that two major processes might be involved: (1) that living in close proximity to members of a disliked racial group would give rise to frequent personal association and to the discovery that individual members of the group did not correspond to the stereotypes about the group but were instead people much like themselves; and (2) that the integrated occupancy pattern would give rise to a perception of social norms, both official (the public authority responsible for the housing project) and unofficial (the other tenants) that favored friendly interracial association. Questions designed to throw light on these two possibilities were therefore included in the interviews in the study. This step was important if the research was to make a contribution to theoretical knowledge or even to be generalizable to situations beyond the specific ones that were studied.

Meanwhile, in the second program of research, the studies reported in *The Authoritarian Personality* also had their original impetus in a concern with a social problem; specifically, with anti-Semitism, or, more generally, with readiness to accept fascist ideology. But the formulation of these studies, unlike the interracial housing study, involved hypotheses drawn directly from an existing body of theory (essentially psychoanalytic) about personality development and the relationship between hostility toward outgroups and other aspects of the individual's personality. Thus the findings were directly relevant to a body of psychological theory but were rather less clear in their implications for solution of the social problems of prejudice and discrimination.

The third program of research, involving another starting point, was the work of Daniel Katz and his associates on the effectiveness of different approaches to changing attitudes of whites toward Blacks. Katz and his colleagues started from a theoretical interest in the various functions that attitudes serve for individuals and in the implications of these differences for the probable success of various approaches to changing attitudes. Although they used attitudes of whites toward Blacks as their subject matter, this topic was not inherent in their problem. In fact, Smith, Bruner, and White (1956), working from a very similar theoretical position, used attitudes toward the Soviet Union as their subject matter. Despite the fact that their starting point was mainly a theoretical one, the findings of Katz and his associates may well have implications for the social problem of reducing prejudice and discrimination.

A. The role of values in the selection of a research topic

Given the great variety of sources that may suggest topics for research, how do investigators select a topic to study? Among the important factors determining choice are the personal inclinations and value judgments of the investigators. It is sometimes thought that "values" have no place in science, but this is a misconception that stems from a failure to distinguish between the selection of a topic to be investigated and the process by which the investigation is carried out.

It is relatively easy to see that investigators' own judgments of value enter into their selection of a research topic when that topic concerns controversial social problems. It is less obvious that the investigators' own values and assumptions are also at work in the selection of such topics as the behavior of rats in a maze under varying conditions, or the physiological and neurological correlates of dreaming, or the effects of various patterns of communication under rigorously controlled experimental conditions. Nevertheless, values are operative in these cases, too. The investigators may value "precision" and "scientific purity"; they may believe that it is more "scientific" to work with "objective" data secured under controlled laboratory conditions than with the less precise data for which one must sometimes settle when studying social phenomena in naturalistic settings.

It would be a mistake, however, to assume that *personal* values are or could be the only determinant in selecting a topic for inquiry. Not only do social conditions under which science is pursued shape the preferences of investigators in subtle and often imperceptible ways, but there are also powerful overt inducements for pursuing research on one topic rather than another. Different societies at different times place premiums on work on different research topics. It may bring more prestige to do research on transplanting human organs than to try to find a cure for the common cold;

more research funds may be available for exploration of outer space than for trying to find solutions for the problems of inner cities; better paid positions may be available for the market researcher than for the educational psychologist. There are few social scientists who can afford to ignore prestige, research funds, and personal income. This state of affairs is likely to result in reducing the effective freedom of choice of research topics. In the United States at the present time, although the number of different sources of research funds is fairly large, a substantial proportion of the money available for research is concentrated in a few government agencies and a few large foundations. As a result, these organizations determine to a considerable extent the problems on which research shall be done. While it is true that the decisions about the broad topics for which research funds will be made available are rather highly centralized, there is frequently considerable flexibility within these broad topics. For example, there is little question that more money is available for research on problems of humans in space than for research in archeology. But a wide variety of problems are considered relevant to space research; these may range all the way from physiological reactions to weightlessness to questions of interpersonal relationships in small groups required to work together in cramped quarters for long periods of time, reactions to prolonged isolation, and methods of selecting individuals best able to withstand both the physiological and psychological stresses involved in space exploration.

B. Values and the outcomes of research

No matter how strongly one's *choice of topic* may be influenced by values, it goes without saying that values should not be allowed to influence the *outcome* of research. Scientists are, of course, human; they would like their research findings to come out in a way that conforms to the way they think the world is, or that fits with the particular theory they have put forward or to which they subscribe, or, at least, that is consistent with findings they have reported earlier. But, as Skinner has pointed out:

> Science is a willingness to accept facts even when they are opposed to wishes. Experiments do not always come out as one expects, but the facts must stand and the expectations fall (1953, pp. 12–13).

What safeguards are there against the intrusion of investigators' wishes and values into the conduct and the results of their research? Some writers believe that the recognition that one's own values are involved serves as one safeguard. Thus, Keniston in *The Uncommitted* (1965, pp. 11–12) has written:

> An attempt to understand individuals in society must confront [an] inevitable problem: the biases, limitations, prejudices, and selectivities of the writer. An American observer of American society inevitably carries a heavy baggage of traditional American assumptions about life; and those who

minimize or deny this imbeddedness in their social and cultural tradition are often its greatest victims. Moreover, the psychologist who tries to understand another individual carries an additional baggage, in the form of his own motivations, selective blindnesses, and favored hypotheses. . . .

This problem cannot be finally solved. My own conviction is that the most truly scientific stratagem in the study of man is a persistent effort to make conscious and explicit one's own motivations and preconceptions; and that the most objective students of society are those whose own values are most clearly stated, not those who claim that "as scientists" they have no values. The major effort of the student of man or society must always be to retain his own openness to his own presuppositions and to what he studies, so that he retains the capacity to be surprised by proving himself wrong. If the writer's preconceptions and values are made explicit, the reader is at least allowed to challenge these assumptions as stated and not required to ferret them out as embedded in "objective" reporting and interpretation.

This constant awareness of the possibility that our own biases may intrude on our research undoubtedly provides some protection. But basically it is the function of scientific method to minimize the likelihood that research findings will be influenced by bias from whatever source, including the investigator's own values. Much of this book consists of a discussion of these methods. The first step is formulating the problem in such a way that it can be investigated by scientific procedures.

II. FORMULATING A SPECIFIC RESEARCH PROBLEM

As we saw in Chapter 2, the selection of a topic for research does not immediately put investigators in a position to start considering what data they will collect, by what methods, and how they will analyze them. Before taking such steps, investigators need to formulate a specific problem that can be investigated by scientific procedures. Unfortunately, it happens not infrequently that investigators attempt to jump immediately from the selection of a topic to the collection of data, violating the logic of analysis discussed in Chapter 2. At best, this means that they will be faced with the task of formulating a problem after the data have been collected; at worst, that they will not produce a scientific inquiry at all.

Beginning researchers, in particular, are likely to find it hard to proceed from the selection of a topic to the spelling out of a specific problem for investigation. Even for experienced investigators this may often be a trying and uncomfortable stage. That it is not always so is in part a simple matter of experience; having even once gone through the trials of formulating a specific problem gives one more of a "feel" both for the difficulties and the ways of overcoming them. More importantly, the outcome of any research usually suggests further questions; thus, if investigators remain interested in the general topic with which they started out, each study they carry out points toward possible succeeding ones.

But what about the beginner—let us say the student trying to develop a researchable thesis problem? What *is* a "researchable problem"? First, the concepts must be clear enough so that one can specify in words exactly what the question is (see Chapter 2). Second, the concepts must be such that they can be represented by some sort of evidence which is obtainable through direct observation or other less direct activities. Third, it must be feasible to carry out such operations or activities.

Let us say that Mr. S., a beginning researcher, has decided that he wants to study aggression, because he considers the understanding and control of aggression vitally important if our society is to survive. He has selected a topic, but it is an extremely broad one. First of all, what does he mean by "aggression"? He may start with some general definition such as "Aggression is any behavior that has the intent of injuring an individual or group." Must the injury be physical? Or may it take the form of making sarcastic remarks, angry accusations, statements likely to humiliate the person or reduce self-esteem or the regard in which the person is held by others? May it take the form of stealing, encroaching upon, or in some way damaging the person's property?

Usually the process of moving from a research topic to a researchable problem involves both a progressive sharpening of concepts and a progressive narrowing of scope. *Progressive* may be a misleading word, if it suggests gradual but steady progress in one direction. Most often the process goes by fits and starts, with sudden exhilarating insights, perhaps equally sudden realizations that one has "progressed" into a blind alley, and long periods when nothing at all seems to be happening and one despairs of ever arriving at a researchable problem—much less carrying out the research.

Let us say the student decides that he is going to limit his topic to physical aggression by one human individual against another. He has narrowed his field considerably but not nearly enough. Does he want to study the effects of different patterns of child rearing on the expression of aggression? Or make a comparative study of the extent to which physical aggression is expected, condoned, or frowned upon in different cultures or subcultures— comparing the Arapesh and the Tchambuli, or street-corner gangs with college professors? Let us say he arrives (somehow) at the decision that he wants to study the conditions under which physical aggression is engaged in by members of cultures or subcultures in which such behavior is usually inhibited. By this time he has very much narrowed his focus; he is close to having a researchable problem. Indeed, if this happened to be an area in which little or no research had been done and there seemed no good basis for setting up even tentative hypotheses about what kinds of conditions stimulate the expression of physical aggression by members of groups in which such behavior is usually inhibited, he might be just about ready to start. That is, he might conclude that so little is known about what conditions are likely to elicit physical aggression on the part of such individuals that a necessary and useful first step would be simply to observe such individuals and record instances of physical aggression as they occurred, taking care to record in detail the circumstances that preceded the aggression, the form it took, its consequences in so far as he could observe them, and any information he could get about the individual who carried out the aggression and the one who was its object (their relative size, for example, or how well they knew each other).

To simplify his life, let us say he decides that middle-class male college students in the United States (or those in the particular college he attends) meet his criteria for his subject population; physical violence is not their usual form of behavior, but it occurs often enough so that, if he were persistent and ingenious in his selection of spots for observation, he might witness and record enough instances of aggression to make possible some categorization of his data on the basis of which he might formulate some tentative hypotheses. (He might, for example, find that more instances of physical aggression occurred in bars than in classrooms, that the rate of physical aggression was higher in connection with protest demonstrations than during registration for courses, and so on).

However, this is a relatively inefficient research procedure, for a number of reasons, not all of which need to be gone into here. Two of the more **dross rate** obvious ones are what Webb, *et al.* (1966) call its high "dross rate" (the amount of observation time during which no incidents of aggression occur), and the fact that the findings are almost certain to be heavily biased in the direction of *public* incidents of aggression. So, if the student is wise, he will try to specify his problem still further. He may find that he can formulate some tentative hypotheses—either on the basis of others' research findings, discussion with friends and colleagues, reflection on his own experience and past unsystematic observations, or just plain "common sense." He may end up with a list of conditions that seem likely to elicit physical aggression on the part of individuals not ordinarily given to such behavior; these might include self-defense against actual or anticipated physical attack or defense of someone else against actual or anticipated attack. And one can add to the list of conditions by extending the definition of aggressive behavior—by defining "aggressive" behavior not as aggression but as a way of influencing another person's behavior either for his own good (for example, spanking a child for running out into a busy street) or for the good of others (spanking a child for hitting another child); by putting the behavior in the context of a contribution to knowledge (for example, as part of an experiment on the effects of negative reinforcements on learning); by putting the behavior in a role-playing context (for example, the individual is asked to take the role of a member of a delinquent gang); and so on.

He cannot very well investigate all of these possibilities in a single study; the task now is to select one or two of them for intensive investigation.

There are no set rules for making this selection. But he may ask himself such questions as the following: Is this problem really *important*? The journals are already cluttered with articles. Will this research make a difference? To whom? Why? Will the research result be *interesting*? Will it be relevant to an idea that has widespread implications? Will it challenge some common-sense truisms or reveal the inadequacies of accepted views? Will the research be *immediately useful*? Will it help to guide or change social policy or practice? Will it provide needed information or new insights into an important social issue?

These are good questions to ask oneself, and if one of the possibilities the students is considering meets these criteria better than the others, the fact should weigh heavily in his decision. However, they should be considered as suggestions, not as absolute requirements. Among graduate students, a frequent barrier to settling on a researchable dissertation problem is the desire to make "a really important contribution"—maybe something that will even revolutionize the field. This is an admirable goal but usually an unrealistic one. Clinging to this goal can immobilize the potential researcher indefinitely. Realistically, one may choose among several possible problems on the basis of his or her own interest, or on the basis of a judgment about which of the hypotheses are most plausible, or which would tie the study most meaningfully into existing knowledge in the area, or, on the other hand, which might make the most novel contribution. Probably the selection is most often (and perhaps most sensibly) made on the basis of the potential investigator's ability to think of ways of putting the possibility into action (that is, of finding operations that correspond to the concepts— a topic that is discussed in detail later).

Our hypothetical student has gone through a rather laborious process in arriving at a researchable problem. Some of this labor is inevitable. But experience has shown that several more systematic approaches are likely to be helpful. These include: careful review of relevant theories and of research already done on the topic; discussion with people who have had experience in the area; first-hand observation; and reflection upon one's own experiences.

A. Review of theory and research already done on the topic

It has become standard that every research report, and especially every thesis or dissertation, starts with a "review of the literature"—sometimes perfunctory, sometimes exhaustive. The fact that this has become almost a routine requirement may blind us to its great potential value in helping to formulate specific research problems. The accumulation of scientific knowledge is a slow, gradual process, in which, on the whole, one group of investigators builds on the work of others and, in turn, contributes their bit or bits, which may then serve as starting points for others. Truly original breakthroughs are rare indeed, and they are the work of geniuses—Galileo,

Newton, Darwin, Freud, Einstein. And, genius notwithstanding, they do not come out of the blue. They are almost always related to prior work—if only by way of challenge and disagreement. An examination of theory and research in the field of one's interest, if it is carried out with an eye for unresolved problems or new applications, may suggest a number of researchable questions that, while not earthshaking, are nevertheless meaningful from the perspective of a gradually accumulating body of scientific knowledge.

1. Reviewing theories that may be relevant

A number of theories are sufficiently well developed so that they have served as the taking-off point for research in the social sciences. Among these are the various learning theories, those theories that explain attitude change as a striving for consistency, role theory, and psychoanalytic theory. There are a number of ways in which reviewing a body of theory may lead to ideas for researchable problems. First, you may think of ways of testing the theory itself or, more likely, specific propositions within it or directly derivable from it. Second, it may suggest an approach to understanding some process or behavior in which you are interested (the development of sympathy, formation of impressions of people, or attitude change, for example). Third, it may suggest a conceptual organization for a mass of data which no other integrating principle seems adequate. As always throughout this book, these are not meant to be sharp distinctions, but rather ranges of gradation.

Since psychoanalytic theory has been used in the formulation of problems in several of the social sciences, we shall use as illustrations three studies deriving from psychoanalytic theory or making use of its hypotheses as major foci in problem formulation. One of the major propositions of psychoanalytic theory is that early experiences—and especially early experiences with respect to the handling of instinctual needs—strongly influence later development. All of the examples we shall use were primarily concerned with this proposition, though in different ways. The first was primarily concerned with testing the proposition; the second made use of the proposition in an attempt to understand a particular problem; the third used a number of specific psychoanalytic propositions in an attempt both to organize a large mass of data and to test the theoretical propositions.

A study primarily concerned with testing the theory.   One of the major difficulties in evaluating the validity of psychoanalytic theory is that its propositions are derived by inference from subjective, retrospective reports of early experience and are not easily checkable by direct observation. During the 1940s, however, there were a number of attempts to test psychoanalytic propositions experimentally by subjecting animals to experiences that might be considered analogous to certain experiences of human infants. One of the most ingenious of these was Hunt's (1941) test of the proposition that deprivation in infancy leads to "miserly" behavior as an adult. Hunt tested this proposition in the laboratory by rearing three groups of rats differently: One group was fed normally during the entire developmental period; the second was fed normally in infancy, scantily during the prepubertal period, then normally again; the third was fed scantily during infancy, but adequately later. In adulthood, all three groups were subjected to a limited diet. When they were subsequently given access to food, only the group that had been deprived in infancy reacted by hoarding pellets of food beyond its immediate needs—the result that would be predicted by psychoanalytic theory. Obviously, Hunt was not interested in hoarding behavior in rats for its own sake; his interest was in an experimental test of a proposition derived from psychoanalytic theory.

A study that used the theory in an attempt to understand a specific problem.   A quite different use of psychoanalytic theory is illustrated by *The Authoritarian Personality* studies (Adorno, *et al.*, 1950). As noted earlier in this chapter, both the study of interracial housing and *The Authoritarian Personality* studies were primarily concerned with the social problems of prejudice and discrimination. Both were carried out in the period during and immediately after World War II, when there was considerable concern that the phenomena that had occurred in Nazi Germany might, under certain conditions, also occur in the United States. Both were intended to yield knowledge that would contribute, directly or indirectly, to understanding and control of racial and religious prejudice.

The group that carried out the interracial housing study selected its major variable—contact with individuals of the disliked group—largely on the empirical ground that people working in the field of intergroup relations had observed that this was frequently an important influence in reducing the prejudice. The idea was not derived from a body of theory; the variable on which the study focused was one of current, adult experience; and although such demographic characteristics as age, religion, and political views were taken into account to some extent, no attempt was made to get information about the personality structure of the individuals in the contact situation. The investigators who carried out *The Authoritarian Personality* studies, on the other hand, taking psychoanalytic theory as their starting point, concentrated on the development of prejudice and authoritarianism in the individual, focusing on such aspects as the person's relationship with his or her parents, the person's attitude toward sex and other instinctual needs, and the function of prejudice both in enhancing one's own ego and in denying one's own unacceptable tendencies by projecting them onto the out-group. While the study could not, by its very nature, provide a conclusive test either of psychoanalytic theory or of its specific hypotheses about the development of prejudice, its general findings were interpreted by the investigators as consistent with the theory, and the study has provided a seemingly inexhaustible source of ideas for subsequent research.

A series of studies concerned both with testing the theory and with using it to integrate a large amount of data in a single explanatory system. Experimental studies with animals, such as Hunt's, are of limited applicability in the testing of psychoanalytic theory; studies resting heavily on the essentially clinical interpretation of retrospective and projective material from individuals, such as *The Authoritarian Personality*, stimulating and insight provoking as they are, do not really meet the conditions for testing theory. Studies that make use of more or less objectively observable and ratable relevant behaviors in a number of different societies provide one of the most effective ways of testing psychoanalytic propositions about the relation of early experience to later development. At the same time, psychoanalytic theory provides a possible approach to organizing a mass of data about various aspects of a society within a single explanatory system. The series of cross-cultural studies carried out by Whiting and his associates may serve as an example of this approach. Although these investigators (Whiting and Child, 1953) stated that they were not concerned with the validity of psychoanalytic theory as such but rather as a source of ideas about the relation between personality development and culture integration, in making use of these ideas they were at least incidentally testing psychoanalytic theory. The first study in this program (Whiting and Child, 1953) focused on the relation between methods of child training in a society and the typical explanations of illness in that society. They considered patterns of training with respect to five areas of behavior that appear universally and are subject to socialization in all societies: oral, anal, sexual, dependent, and aggressive. Making the assumption that explanations of illness (at least in prescientific societies) tend to be projective, they predicted that the more anxiety provoking the method of training with respect to a given area of behavior, the more likely it was that the society would attribute illness to events associated with that behavior area; for example, that in societies where weaning of infants is abrupt and harsh, beliefs about sickness will tend to attribute it to some type of oral activity. This hypothesis was supported with respect to the oral, dependent, and aggressive areas of behavior. In another study in this research program (Whiting, Kluckhohn, and Anthony, 1958), it was hypothesized that the more exclusive the relationship between son and mother in the early years of life, the more severe the male initiation rites at puberty were likely to be; this hypothesis too was supported. In still another study (Whiting, 1959) it was found that methods of social control of adult behavior were related to methods of child rearing, as follows: (1) Belief in and use of sorcery (considered by the investigator to represent paranoid fear of retaliation from other humans) will be strongest in societies where there is an early intimate or seductive relationship between mother and infant, followed by severe punishment for sexual behavior later; (2) belief in and dread of punishment by gods or ghosts (considered as a projection of a sense of sin) will be strongest in societies where there is neglect during infancy, followed by severe punishment for aggressive behavior later; (3) a sense of personal responsibility for wrong-doing (guilt) will be strongest in societies where child training is begun early, and where the family pattern is one of monogamous marriage with only the immediate nuclear family living in a household.

The focus in these studies is not on individuals but on societies; by making use of the large amount of descriptive anthropological material that has been gathered in the Human Relations Area Files at Yale University, the relationships among two or more variables may be studied in a large number of societies. If the relationships are found to hold in many societies, regardless of the great variety of specific ways in which a given variable may be manifested in different societies, this helps both to understand the relationships among variables within any given society and to support the basic theory from which the predictions about relationships are derived. In particular, with respect to psychoanalytic theory, cross-cultural studies such as this help to sort out which aspects of the theory represent experiences specific to middle-class Jewish Viennese society at the end of the nineteenth century; which aspects represent more or less universal experiences; and which aspects of the theory need modification in order to account for relationships observed in other societies.

2. Reviewing research

Reviewing research already done on the topic in which you are interested may help in the formulation of a specific problem through many different processes. We shall consider illustrations of a number of these: challenging the findings or interpretation of prior research; attempting to clarify the processes underlying the findings of previous research; repeating earlier studies to see if their findings hold up; extending earlier research into new areas or to cover new phenomena; attempting to account for unexpected results or failure to confirm prediction; seeing a way of applying the methods used in studying one problem to investigate another problem for which appropriate methods have not been available; seeing unusual ways of combining earlier work in two different areas to produce a new approach to a problem.

Challenging prior research. A well-known study that had its origin in a challenge to earlier research is Asch's (1958) investigation of conformity to judgments of others. During the 1930s and 1940s, a great deal of research had been done on the effects of social norms on various kinds of behavior, with the general finding being one of considerable conformity on the part of individuals. The classic study in this area was that by Sherif (1936), which made use of the so-called autokinetic phenomenon—the fact that a stationary light, seen against a background of complete darkness, appears to move. Sherif had subjects make judgments of the distance the light moved. In one condition, each individual, tested alone, made a large number of such judgments until he had arrived at a fairly stable judgment; then two or three individuals were placed together, and each made his judgments aloud. In another condition, individuals worked at first in groups of two or three, making judgments aloud, and then were separated and asked to make the judgments as individuals. In both conditions, the clear finding was that individuals' judgments were strongly influenced by those of others, though they might not be aware of this influence or of the change in their own judgments. Asch (1958) did not question the *findings* of this and similar studies; he did, however, question the conclusions drawn from them, on the ground that specific aspects of the experimental procedures influenced the outcomes. In particular, he argued that the use of ambiguous stimuli (for example, lights that appeared to move, against a background that offered no possible objective basis for an estimate of how far they moved) favored the outcome of "slavish submission" to the judgments of others. He suggested that if subjects were presented with stimuli about which they could make clear objective judgments, the frequently found "conformity effects" would be very much reduced. He therefore presented subjects with sets of three lines differing in length and asked them to judge which of the three was the same length as a fourth line. That the judgments could be made clearly and without difficulty was shown by a pretest in which individuals, tested alone, made the judgments almost without error. In Asch's experimental situation, however, the judgments were made in groups, in which all but one of the members were confederates of the experimenter and were instructed to give incorrect replies on specified trials. The results were not entirely in keeping with Asch's expectation. Although in roughly two-thirds of the judgments the subjects gave the correct answer in spite of the unanimous wrong answers of the experimental confederates, one-third of the judgments erred in the direction of agreeing with the judgments given by the confederates, even though these were patently wrong.

Clarifying underlying processes. Reviewing previous research may often turn up instances of interesting findings that one sees no reason to challenge, but in which the process underlying the findings is not entirely clear and seems worth clarifying. It may be a single study, or a series of related studies, or a large number of otherwise unrelated studies on a particular topic that have a common finding. There may be a variety of reasons for the ambiguity about the underlying process. In some instances it may be clear that one factor or set of factors is influencing some outcome, but the components of the factors may be so closely intertwined that it is impossible to judge their relative importance in determining the outcome. But you may see some way of "untying" the components so that their separate contributions to the outcome can be measured. In other instances the work done so far may have demonstrated rather clearly a relationship between two variables, but it may be ambiguous as to whether condition X tends to lead to condition Y, or vice versa, or whether some other condition or set of conditions tends to produce both of them. In such a case, you may see some way of throwing light on the nature of the relationship.

Let us then present an example of a "classic" study that distinguished the components of a variable that had previously been treated as an undifferentiated whole. During the 1940s Kurt Lewin and his associates carried out a series of studies all of which had the clear finding that "group decision" was more effective than lecturing or other information-giving procedures in leading people to change their behavior—whether it was buying cuts of meat not ordinarily used, feeding their infants recommended amounts of orange juice and cod liver oil, or changing production methods in a factory. But Bennett (1955) recognized that several different aspects were lumped together under the heading of "group decision"; these included not only group discussion, but an explicit request by the leader at the end of the discussion for a decision about either individual or group action and for an explicit public indication of intention to carry out the action. Moreover, this public indication (usually by raising hands or some similar technique) not only meant that individuals had committed themselves in front of others, but that they had an opportunity to observe how many others in the group had also committed themselves to the action. Noting that all of these features could be part of a lecture as well as of a group discussion, Bennett set up an experiment in which the following four variables were separately identified and systematically combined in appealing for volunteer subjects for experiments: group discussion versus lecture (on the need for subjects and the importance of research); an explicit request for each individual to decide whether he or she would volunteer versus no such request; a request that the commitment be made publicly versus allowing it to remain private; and, finally, information about the number of people in the group who had agreed to volunteer. She found that neither the group discussion nor the publicness of the commitment were essential; asking individuals to make an explicit decision at the time as to whether or not they would volunteer, and providing information that led them to believe that most of the others in the class had decided to do so, proved to be the determining factors in the number of students volunteering and actually showing up at the appointed time. Bennett was therefore able to reformulate the rather vague statement that group decision is more effective than a lecture in getting people to change their behavior, to a more specific statement about a decision about individual goals in a setting of shared norms about such goals.

Repeating an earlier study to see if its findings hold up. Any piece of research must be repeated by other investigators before its findings can be considered as reasonably well established. In the physical sciences, this **replication** typically means repetition (or, to use the technical term, replication) under the same conditions, using identical procedures. Exact replications of studies are occasionally carried out in the social sciences as well; more often, however, there is some variation, introduced in order to clarify the meaning of the findings or to provide a different kind of evidence to represent the underlying concepts (this point will be discussed in detail later), or both. In practice, of course, not all studies are repeated, either in identical form or with modifications. Of the thousands of studies that have been done, how do you select which ones are worth redoing in order to see if you would get the same findings, even though you have no specific reason for challenging them? The usual criterion is that the problem is recognized as important, and the findings have such great potential significance either for theory or for practice, or both, that it seems worth checking them for added confirmation.

The work of the Swiss psychologist Jean Piaget is of this sort, and there have been innumerable studies whose major purpose was to see if his findings held up in other countries. We shall consider his work on moral judgment, and some of the studies designed to check his findings, as examples. In 1932, *The Moral Judgment of the Child* was published. In it, Piaget reported a series of studies, some of which involved playing games (especially marbles) with children and asking them about the rules, others of which involved informal interviews in which Piaget told the child about an incident involving some moral issue of "right" or "wrong" and asked for the child's opinion. He concluded that moral judgment develops in a sequential process, with three major stages: young children see adult rules as sacred, unchangeable things; at about the age of eight, children begin to shift toward regarding rules as products of group agreement and as instruments for achieving cooperative purposes. In the early part of this stage, the concept of reciprocity dominates, with regard to both reward and punishment; one behaves in certain ways in exchange for corresponding behavior from others (for example, taking turns in using desired equipment), and punishment is of the "eye for an eye" variety. Later in this stage, this simple conception of equity is modified in the direction of relativism, taking into account the specific circumstances, the intention of the wrongdoer, and other considerations. From these observations Piaget concluded that moral judgment is not taught but, rather, develops spontaneously from children's attempts to make sense of the social interactions in their world, and that the more mature stages develop from each child's interactions with other children rather than with adults.

Clearly, the question is an important one. Piaget's conclusions conflicted not only with the common-sense view that children must be *taught* what is "right" and what is "wrong," but also with the psychological theories dominant at the time: learning theory, which holds that the development of morality is essentially a matter of conditioning, with positive and negative reinforcement impressing the desired patterns of behavior; and psychoanalytic theory, which holds that conscience develops as children resolve the Oedipal conflict by identifying with the same-sex parent and internalizing their standards.

Within five years, Lerner (1937) had repeated Piaget's study in the United States, using the same hypothetical situations Piaget had presented to his subjects and also getting information about areas of constraint and permissiveness in parental discipline, to test Piaget's speculation that the strictness or permissiveness of parental discipline might affect the rate of development of moral judgment, though not the basic pattern of development. In general, he found the same sequence of development reported by Piaget, but the nature of parental discipline seemed to have little bearing on it.

In succeeding years, Piaget's study was repeated—sometimes using the same hypothetical incidents, sometimes different ones—in Belgium, England, and Spain. Except for the Lerner study described above, there was at first little interest in the United States in Piaget's work. However, in the 1950s and 1960s it received a good deal of attention, and a number of studies were based on it. One investigator (Durkin, 1959) stated explicitly the reason for replicating Piaget's work. She wrote:

> [This investigation] is specifically designed to examine developmental trends, with age, in [children's concepts of justice] and to compare the trends with those described by Piaget in *The Moral Judgment of the Child.* . . . If subjects different in nationality and economic status from those included in the Piaget study, but similar in terms of chronological age, were questioned about an act of physical aggression, would their responses reflect stages in moral judgment identical to those outlined by Piaget? Or has he, on the basis of interviews with children "from the poorer parts of Geneva (Switzerland)," made too sweeping generalizations about children in general? (1959, p. 60)

How many replications of a given study are needed? Presumably there comes a point where simple replications bring diminishing returns; either the findings have been fairly well substantiated, or the hypothesis has been rather clearly disconfirmed. However, if the problem is considered an important one and the initial work is sufficiently provocative, variations may be introduced in order to clarify some aspect of the findings or their theoretical implications, to test how far they can be extended, or to investigate the influence of factors not included in the original study. This has happened with respect to Piaget's work. Subsequent investigators, using his basic approach, have compared the development of moral judgment in children of different socioeconomic classes, in children of the same chronological age but differing in IQ, of children differing in the extent of their participation in groups their own age, and in both boys and girls. Other investigators have focused on the content of the issues presented to the children, analyzing responses to determine whether moral judgment is essentially unitary or whether there are distinct factors within it, and whether the development may be conceptualized better in terms of a number of subtypes rather than as maturing along a single line. In recent years, investigators have used techniques rather different from Piaget's, still with the purpose of checking his findings and the conclusions he drew from them. For example, Turiel (1964) did not simply present children with hypothetical incidents and record their replies, as Piaget had done; he presented them also with solutions representing varying levels of maturity of moral judgment. He found that children accept moral reasoning one level above their own functioning stage to a much greater extent than moral reasoning two levels above their own functioning stage; he also found that children accepted moral reasoning one stage lower than their own. These findings tend to support Piaget's conclusion that moral judgment develops according to a rather invariant sequence. On the whole, the considerable body of research on the development of moral judgment stemming from Piaget's work has supported his basic conclusion, though not all of his specific findings. The increasing variety of research techniques applied to checking Piaget's findings and his interpretation of them testifies to the fact that a single piece of research, if it deals with an important problem and if its findings are sufficiently provocative, may provide the starting point for many studies over a considerable period of time. Its possibilities for stimulating new formulations are not exhausted by one or two subsequent studies.

Testing whether a relationship found in one area extends to another area. In the examples of replication given above, the major purpose of the later studies was to check the findings of an earlier one. To be sure, different settings were used, but they were intended to represent essentially the same concepts as the earlier studies. In the present category, the intention is not simply to confirm, or clarify, or qualify, the earlier findings, but to test whether they extend to situations that differ in their conceptual structure as well as in their specific details. The question of the effects of personal contact with members of a social group different from one's own on one's attitudes toward that group provides examples of both kinds of study. In the study of public housing discussed at the beginning of this chapter, it was found that white housewives living in racially integrated housing projects had more contact with Blacks in the projects and more favorable attitudes toward them than did white housewives living in segregated biracial projects. Some questions were raised about the interpretation and generalizability of the findings of that study; they centered around possible differences in the over-all racial climate in the two cities where the projects were located, and also around specific aspects of the occupancy pattern and the proportions of white and Black tenants in the projects. A replication of the study was carried out by members of the same research group (Wilner, Walkley, and Cook, 1955). This second study was still concerned with the effects of occupancy pattern on the relations between white and Black tenants in public housing projects. But it differed from the first study mainly in that the cities in which the integrated and segregated projects were located were more carefully matched, the pattern of segregation in the segregated projects was less extreme, and the proportion of Blacks in the projects was lower—all of these differences having essentially the function of providing checks and clarification of the findings of the earlier study. When this second study also found that white housewives who lived relatively close to a Black family had more contact with Blacks in the project and were more favorable toward them than white housewives within the same projects who lived farther from any of the Black tenants, the group felt that their findings had been reasonably well established with respect to the effects of residential proximity on the behavior and attitudes of white housewives toward Blacks in public housing projects in the United States.

They wondered, however, how general the principles and processes were. In the early 1950s, when international exchange of students was rapidly increasing, a number of foundations made available funds for the study of cross-cultural education and invited social scientists to submit research proposals. The group saw in this an opportunity to test whether their findings about the effects of situational variables on personal contact between members of different social groups, and the effect of such contact on attitudes, held true under conditions that differed not only in specific details but in more basic ways. They recognized, for example, that their studies, and, in fact, most of the research that had been done on this question in the United States, focused on the behavior and attitudes of members of the dominant white majority toward ethnic groups against whom there was a good deal of prejudice. In the cross-cultural study that they proposed, the focus was quite different; it was on the effects of contact on the attitudes of foreign students toward United States citizens. The researchers found that one aspect of their earlier findings did not hold up: The extent of contact with United States citizens seemed to have no consistent effect on favorableness or unfavorableness of attitudes toward them.

Attempting to account for unexpected findings or failure to confirm predictions. Unexpected findings, or failure to confirm a prediction or hypothesis, may provide a fruitful starting point for subsequent research. In fact, the long and brilliant program of research by Harlow and his associates (Harlow, 1959; Harlow, 1962; Seay, Alexander, and Harlow, 1964) on the effects of social deprivation on the development of affection in monkeys seems to have grown out of a series of such incidents. According to Harlow's own report, a carefully planned program to establish experimental neuroses in infant monkeys by having them live with unfriendly and inconsistent mother surrogates failed. These surrogate mothers were not real monkeys but contraptions of various sorts: one periodically threw "her" infant from her when a wire frame embedded in her spun-nylon covering was displaced violently upward and backward; another had a series of nozzles down the center of her body which released compressed air under high pressure; another shook her infant so violently that its teeth chattered. In each case, the infant monkey clung to the mother surrogate, showed signs of affection for it, and showed no neurotic symptoms. Concurrently, however, in an effort to produce sturdy and disease-free animals for use in various research programs, a number of infant monkeys were separated from their mothers at birth and placed in individual cages where they were carefully tended but in which they had no direct contact with other monkeys. Eventually the investigators realized that these monkeys were showing all sorts of neurotic behavior: staring fixedly into space, clutching their heads in both hands and rocking back and forth, biting themselves in apparent fury. As Harlow (1962, p. 6) puts it: "We had failed to produce neurotic monkeys by thoughtful planning and creative research, but we had succeeded in producing neurotic monkeys through misadventure."

This observation led to a study of the mother-infant affectional bond, focusing on an attempt to find out what specific aspects of the interaction between mother and infant led to the development of security and affection. In particular, the investigators were interested in the relative importance of the mother as a source of food versus her importance as a source of comfortable bodily contact. In this study (Harlow, 1959), infant monkeys were separated from their mothers at birth and were provided with surrogate mothers—again not real monkeys, but inanimate contraptions. One was a wire cylindrical form with a wooden head, with the nipple of a feeding bottle protruding from its "breast"; the other was the same form covered with terry cloth. None of these monkeys had contact with any other monkeys, either the same age or adults, during the first two months of their lives. Early results suggested that the terry-cloth mothers were adequate substitutes for real mothers; the infants clung to them and ran to them when they were frightened or after a period of separation, while those raised on the wire forms behaved like the monkeys raised in complete isolation. Harlow (1959) concluded that "contact comfort" was the important element in the development of the "love" of an infant monkey for its mother.

However, when these monkeys reached sexual maturity, it became apparent that their social and sexual behavior was grossly aberrant; neither the males nor the females engaged in normal sexual behavior. Moreover, the few females who eventually bore infants were grossly inadequate as mothers. These outcomes led to further research on the effects of varying degrees, periods, and kinds of social deprivation: complete isolation, in cages with wire walls through which the monkey could see and hear other monkeys but had no physical contact with them; different lengths of isolation, ranging from eighty days to a year; and isolation from the mother versus isolation from monkeys the same age. On the basis of these studies, the investigators concluded that there is a critical period of development during which social experience is necessary for normal behavior in later life, and—unexpectedly —that contact with the other monkeys of the same age during the growing-up period is more important to social and sexual development than is contact with the mother and may, in fact, make up for deprivation of maternal care. However, they noted that this latter conclusion was tentative, since at the time of reporting these monkeys were about two years old; whether deprivation of a real mother during infancy would affect their later social adjustment or their maternal behavior remained to be seen.

This program of research demonstrates that unexpected results or failure to confirm a hypothesis, far from being catastrophic, may serve as the basis for highly ingenious and imaginative research. Moreover, from the point of view of the student trying to formulate a research problem, this approach has one limitation. Investigators do not usually publish such findings until they themselves have done further research to try to understand them. Thus the opportunity to formulate a problem on this basis is likely to be available only to those in a situation where there has been some unexpected outcome that can serve as the takeoff point for new research.

Seeing how techniques developed for one problem may be applied to the investigation of a different problem. Asch's (1958) study of the effects of group pressure on judgments of the length of lines has been followed by innumerable studies, which varied the stimuli being judged (for example, using statements of opinion and agree-disagree responses rather than judgments of objective stimuli), the conditions under which judgments are expressed (for example, aloud in the presence of others versus privately in writing), and so on; but all of them investigated the same basic problem—conformity to group norms. Milgram (1961), however, saw in Asch's technique a way of investigating a quite different problem—differences in "national character." Throughout the ages, travelers have been struck by differences in customs from one country to another, and it has also seemed to them that the people of one country differ from those of another in basic personality characteristics as well as in more superficial behavior. Even after the social sciences began to develop, the question of differences in national character remained largely a matter of speculation rather than systematic research, except for studies by cultural anthropologists of small, usually preliterate societies.

Among the reasons for this paucity of research were the complexity of the problem and the lack of adequate techniques for investigating it. Milgram saw in Asch's technique an objective method for investigating a frequently made statement about differences among the citizens of various Western countries—specifically, that people in the United States tend to be highly conformist, people in France nonconformist. He carried out replications of Asch's study with college students in France and, as an added comparison, in Norway—not with the purpose of testing the universality of Asch's findings but as an objective way of testing heretofore impressionistic statements about a difference in national character. Comparing his results with Asch's, he found that they were consistent with the impressionistic statements: French students yielded to the inaccurate judgments of the group of confederates much less often than did United States students; Norwegian students were intermediate. Milgram recognized, of course, that the students in his experiments could not be considered as representative samples of the people of their countries; he pointed out, however, that this was true also of Asch's study with respect to people in the United States. Despite this limitation, Milgram's study demonstrated the possibility of applying objective experimental methods from one study to the investigation of a previously speculative question.

III. DEFINING CONCEPTS AND DECIDING ON OPERATIONS TO REPRESENT THEM

Any group of investigators, in order to organize their data so that they may perceive relationships among them, must make use of concepts. As we indi-

concept cated in Chapter 2, a concept is an abstraction from observed events, or, as McClelland (1951) has defined it, "a shorthand representation of a variety of facts. Its purpose is to simplify thinking by subsuming a number of events under one general heading." Some concepts are quite close to the objects or facts they represent. Thus, for example, the meaning of the concept *dog* may be easily illustrated by pointing to specific dogs. The concept is an abstraction of the characteristics all dogs have in common— characteristics that are either directly observable or easily measured. Other concepts, however, cannot be so easily related to the phenomena they are intended to represent; "political attitude," "role," "job motivation," "democracy" are of this sort. They are inferences, at a higher level of abstraction from concrete events, and their meaning cannot easily be conveyed by pointing to specific objects, individuals, or events. Sometimes these higher-

constructs level abstractions are referred to as constructs, since they are *constructed* from concepts at a lower level of abstraction. The greater the distance between one's concepts, or constructs, and the empirical facts or activities to which they are intended to refer, the greater the possibility of their being misunderstood or carelessly used, and the greater the care that must be given to defining them.

Definitions of concepts and the appropriateness of the operations used to represent them have been central issues in many of the examples of problem formulation given in the preceding section, especially those problems that used prior research as their starting point. For a more detailed discussion of these steps, however, let us return to the hypothetical student, Mr. S, we discussed earlier, interested in the conditions under which physical aggression is engaged in by members of cultures or subcultures in which such behavior is usually inhibited.

Let us say that the student has tentatively decided to investigate the hypothesis that members of such groups are more likely to engage in aggressive behavior if it is put in the context of a contribution to knowledge.

There are two abstract concepts here: "aggressive behavior" and "contribution to knowledge." The student researcher must be clear about what he means by each of them, both in order to relate his findings to other research and as a basis for deciding what operations seem appropriate to represent them.

The student researcher has earlier defined *aggression* as "any behavior that has the intent of injuring an individual or group" and has further specified that he is concerned with physical aggression by one human being against another, thus ruling out purely verbal attacks and attacks against inanimate objects or animals. On a common-sense basis, this may seem like an adequate definition of his concept. But there is an important aspect that must be considered before he can decide on operations by means of which to test his hypothesis. How important is *intent* in his definition of aggression? Would accidental injury to another human being be included in his definition of aggression? Probably not. Would behavior that is intended to produce physical harm be included in his definition even if it does not in fact have that consequence? Probably yes. Is behavior carried out with the knowledge that it will probably inflict pain, even though that is not its major purpose, to be considered aggressive? For example, how about a doctor administering a painful injection? Is there an implication of motivation; that is, does *aggression* presuppose anger, hostility, frustration, or some similar emotional state? If his concept of aggression does involve some such motivational state, his research procedures must include some operation designed to ensure that his subjects are likely to be made to feel angry. If his concept does not involve motivation of this sort, where does he draw the line between *aggression* and knowingly inflicting pain or injury in the pursuit of some other goal?

Since there has been a great deal of research on the topic of aggression, he would do well to review it, paying careful attention to the definitions, explicit or implicit, that other investigators have used. He will find, however, that different investigators have differed to some extent in their concepts of aggression, particularly with regard to the issues of intent and motivation. He must still specify his own definition, but knowing the definitions others have used will help him both to clarify his own concept and, later, to relate his findings to those of other investigators.

"Contribution to knowledge" is probably a less tricky concept, but the researcher may do well to consider whether the particular kind of knowledge to be gained must seem important to the subjects—that is, whether his concept requires that the subjects as well as the investigator see their behavior as contributing to some worthwhile knowledge. For example, if the knowledge allegedly to be gained has to do with increasing the efficiency of military operations, will it constitute a "contribution" in the eyes of subjects who may be pacifists?

No matter how simply or how elaborately we as investigators formally define our concepts, we must find some way of translating them into observable events if we are to carry out any research. That is, we must set up "working definitions." If our hypothetical student has decided, for example, that intent or motivation to harm another person is part of his concept of aggression, he must devise some way of finding subjects who are likely to be "feeling aggressive" (perhaps members of an athletic team who have just lost an important game, or pickets demonstrating against some factory policy, or participants in a demonstration who have just been arrested), or of inducing such feelings in his subjects (by treating them rudely, perhaps, or having them watch a movie filled with scenes of violence).

He must also decide what kinds of behavior he is going to accept as representing aggression. A mother or teacher slapping a child? One man punching another? A subject in an experimental laboratory administering electric shock to another? In our example, one basis for deciding what kinds of behavior to use as indicators of aggression would be the plausibility of the argument that the behavior in question would contribute to knowledge, since contribution to knowledge has been selected as the condition whose effect on the expression of aggression is to be investigated. Will the subjects be told that the investigation is concerned with the effects of punishment on learning? Such an explanation might plausibly be given as the reason for asking subjects to serve as "teachers" in a laboratory experiment and to administer electric shocks when the "learners" did not respond correctly. Conceivably, mothers might be induced to slap their children when they misbehaved, on the ground that the investigation was concerned with the effects of various ways of expressing disapproval of children's undesirable behavior. Or might the alleged knowledge to be gained have to do with the tolerance of pain under the influence of hypnosis? Administering electric shocks in a laboratory would be plausible in relation to such an explanation; slapping one's child would probably not be.

Suppose the investigator decides that direct physical aggression against another human being is too improper to work with. Can he use some milder form of aggressive behavior and still have it relevant to his concepts? How about allowing (or encouraging) children to hit a punching bag? This might well be considered an adequate representation of the concept of aggressive behavior, but it would be difficult to relate to the other concept involved in the hypotheses—making a contribution to knowledge. How about asking subjects to check how much punishment they would be willing to inflict under various conditions—one of the conditions, of course, is taking part in a study of the effects of punishment on learning? Making a check mark on a scale of intensity of punishment one would be willing to inflict is a considerable distance from slapping a child or pushing the button that administers an electric shock. Is it an adequate working definition of aggressive behavior?

Working definitions are adequate if the instruments or procedures based on them gather data that constitute satisfactory indicators of the concepts they are intended to represent. Whether this result has been achieved is often a matter of judgment. Investigators may feel that their data provide reasonably good indicators of their concepts; a critic of the study may feel that they do not. It frequently happens that investigators themselves are aware that their data constitute only a very limited reflection of the concept they have in mind, but, especially in the early stages of research on a problem, they may not be able to devise a more satisfactory one. In any case, although investigators usually report their findings in relation to their abstract concepts in order to relate them more readily to other research and to theory, they and their readers must keep in mind that what they have actually found is a relationship between two sets of data or of operations that are intended to *represent* their concepts.

IV. RELATING THE STUDY TO OTHER KNOWLEDGE

Regardless of the basis on which the problem has been formulated, it is a good idea to recheck research already done and any theoretical writing that may be relevant. You may discover that, even if your initial review of theory and research did not give you any ideas for a researchable problem, now that you have arrived at one, some of the earlier work is relevant to it. If this turns out to be the case, it has a number of advantages. For one thing, it may help you to clarify your problem still further. For another, it may suggest ways of translating your concepts into concrete operations. Finally, it can help ensure that your findings will make a contribution to a body of knowledge. Scientific research is a community enterprise, even though single studies are frequently carried out by individual investigators working alone. In general, each study rests on earlier ones and provides a basis for future ones. The more links that can be established between a given study and other studies or a body of theory, the greater the probable contribution.

The relation between theory and research is discussed in some detail in Chapter 2. However, the point is brought up here because it is important to consider, as we plan a study, ways in which it can be brought into relation to a larger body of knowledge. If the question of relating the findings to other knowledge is not considered until *after* the study is carried out and the report is being written, you may find that, although you have carried out a study that is adequate in itself, you have not built in provisions which, if they had been included, would have increased the contribution of your study to a larger store of knowledge.

A major way of ensuring that your study will be relevant to other knowledge is, of course, formulating it in relation to prior research or theory. Another way of relating a study to a larger body of knowledge is to formulate the research problem at a level sufficiently abstract so that findings of the study may be related to findings of other studies concerned with the same concepts. Studies that arise from the need to answer a practical question may remain at such a specific level that they make no real contribution to knowledge unless the investigator takes pains to transpose the question to a higher level of abstraction.

Let us consider the example of a group of investigators who are asked by an agency concerned with conserving environmental resources to carry out a survey to evaluate the effectiveness of a series of cartoons. These cartoons have been designed for use in a campaign to make the public aware of various aspects of this issue. If the researchers set up the problem in such a way that they cannot generalize beyond the specific cartoons in question, they will fail in both their scientific *and* their practical assignment. The cartoons they are about to investigate are unique products and to some extent different from all other cartoons in content and form. If they set the research process in motion in order to determine the effectiveness of these few cartoons, which may be topical today and forgotten tomorrow, they are involved in a task that will have to begin again as soon as it is finished. If they discover, for example, that a specific cartoon attracts and amuses a part of its audience but is misunderstood by the majority, they have learned little that deserves to be classified as scientific knowledge. Nor can such results provide much guidance for the cartoon producer. In order to remove this limitation on their work, the investigators, before they proceed to collect data, must reformulate their concrete problem in a manner that will ultimately permit them to draw conclusions about the more general aspects of both the cartoons themselves and the responses of persons exposed to them. In other words, their concern, in this stage of problem formulation, must be with the generalizability of their results. It is not enough to ask whether one or more particular cartoons are understood. Rather, they must ask, for each cartoon: What aspects of the cartoon are understood—and by whom? To be able to answer the first part of the question, they must analyze the general features of the cartoon. They may emerge with categories such as "satire," "caption required for understanding," and so on. If they can then demonstrate through their inquiry that this type of cartoon is misunderstood because it is taken literally instead of satirically, they are in a position to advise the artist to experiment either with nonsatirical cartoons or with ways of making the satire clearer. To be able to answer the second part of the question, they must consider what characteristics of the viewers are likely to be relevant to their understanding of the cartoons—for example, their educational level, their general political orientation, and their awareness of problems of pollution and conservation. If the organization is especially interested in reaching some particular target group, the investigators can then advise them as to what kinds of cartoons are most likely to be effective with that group.

Sometimes the difficulty in relating research focused on a particular situation to a larger body of knowledge arises from the fact that in any given setting so many variables may be at work that it is hard to judge which ones may be the links to more general principles. Consider, for example, two doctoral dissertations. One, by a supervisor of nurses in a hospital in a south-central state, found that the white nurses-in-training became more favorable in their attitude toward Blacks after they had worked on wards where many of the patients were Black (and on welfare). The other, by the director of a tutorial program in a northwestern state, in which white students at a school of education tutored Black high school students, found that, after the tutorial experience, the white students who had tutored Blacks were less prejudiced than a comparison group of white students who had not had this experience. Each of these findings is of interest in its own setting, but neither, by itself, seems to contribute much to the already considerable body of research on the effects of contact on the attitudes of whites toward Blacks. Taken together, however, they suggest a qualification of a princple that has been considered rather well documented: that, to lead to more favorable attitudes on the part of whites toward Blacks, the contact situation must be such that the Black and white participants have equal status within it. But in both of these studies the whites are in some sense in a superior status. Taking either study alone, there are so many other possible influences that it would be difficult to single out any one even tentatively as the most likely explanation of this apparent variation from the general findings. But the two together suggest that when the superior status involves *helping* the other person, its effects are different than when this aspect is not present. Single studies that do not seem to add anything new to the general store of knowledge, beyond the particular situation in which they were carried out, are often not published; thus the opportunity for pulling together such findings into a generalizable principle may be missed. This fact points again to the importance of checking sources of unpublished research, such as data archives and dissertation abstracts.

V. DETERMINING THE FEASIBILITY OF THE PROJECT

Earlier in the chapter three criteria were suggested for determining whether a problem, as formulated, is researchable: The meaning of the concepts must be clear, they must be represented by some evidence which is obtainable through direct observation or other less direct activities, and it must be feasible to carry out the necessary observations or activities. Consideration of all these aspects, and many others, goes on simultaneously. As we define our concepts and mull over possible operations to represent them, we are almost of necessity thinking of possible settings for our research, what kinds of subjects would be appropriate, and how we will collect and analyze our data.

In the discussion of ways of going about formulating researchable problems, issues of clarifying concepts and finding appropriate ways of getting evidence about them have necessarily come up, but for the most part incidentally, in the course of illustrating how one or another set of investigators determined their research problem. Different kinds of research problems differ considerably in the issues they raise about definition of concepts and operations representing them; thus these issues will be discussed in the next chapters, in relation to specific kinds of problems and research designs. Obviously, questions of feasibility also vary with different problems, activities, and research designs; nevertheless, there are enough common aspects to make a general discussion of feasibility appropriate at this point. To some extent, questions of feasibility are matters of common sense, but they also involve experience; there are all sorts of pitfalls of which the beginner is likely to be unaware but about which an experienced investigator can offer caution.

A. The scope of the problem

Most beginners tend to select too big a problem with too many variables; it is important to set limits on how much one tries to cover in a single study. In a sense, this theme has run through all of the preceding sections, but it has not always been made explicit. Let us go back to the example of the student wanting to study conditions under which people who do not ordinarily engage in physical aggression against another person may do so. We listed half a dozen possible conditions; any reasonably ingenious reader could probably list half a dozen more. But even if one could think of operations to represent each of these conditions, it would be practically impossible to study them all at once; the research project would be much too unwieldy. It is impossible to give any set rule as to how many variables can reasonably be investigated in a single study; but if the variables are at all complicated, and if they involve any manipulation by the investigator, it is usually not feasible to investigate more than two or three in a given study. The investigator must select the ones that seem most likely to be important or for which reasonable operations can most readily be found. The investigator may plan to investigate the effects of some of the other variables in later studies, but the first one should be of manageable size and set up in such a way that it can stand by itself.

B. Time

Most researchers would agree with a general "law" of research that says: "Things take more time than you think they will." This "law" applies at every stage of every investigation. By the time the student has arrived at the point of trying to work out a reasonable time plan for his study, he will probably already have discovered that it has taken him about ten times as long as he would have supposed to develop a researchable problem, with clearly defined concepts and operations. It may be possible to estimate the time for subsequent stages somewhat more realistically, but each one will almost certainly take longer than most of us would reasonably expect. Consider the following very incomplete list.

1. How long will it take to recruit a sufficient number of appropriate subjects?
2. If instruments are needed, either for manipulation of variables or for measurement of outcomes, are they available? If not, how long will it take to develop them? If they are available, does it take time to learn how to use them? These questions apply both to physical equipment and to measures such as questionnaires, projective tests, and so on.
3. Once all the preliminaries have been worked out, how long will the actual data collection take? For example, can it be carried out with subjects in large groups, or does it call for small groups, or individual sessions with each subject? Is it a "one-shot" affair, or does it require repeated exposures or testing over an extended period of time? If it is a survey-type study involving a specified sample, how much extra time must be allowed for return visits to people who were not at home on the interviewer's first visit (or the second, or the third)? If it is an experimental laboratory study, how much extra time must be allowed for replacing subjects who fail to show up—especially if it is a small-group study in which the absence of one subject makes it impossible to carry out the operations and thus makes it necessary to reschedule not only the missing subject but the others assigned to the same group?
4. How long will it take to process the data? If it consists of continuous observational records, unstructured interviews, or similar data, it may take a long time to set up codes, achieve reliability of coding, and then actually code the data. If it involves computer analysis, is an appropriate computer program available?
5. How long will it take to write the report?

C. Money

Many of the questions about financial costs are similar to those about time. For everything that is not done by the investigators themselves, time is likely to mean money. And, of course, there may be (and usually are) expenses that go beyond simply paying for time. Again, here is a list of questions to consider.

1. Will it be necessary to pay subjects?
2. If equipment is not available but can be bought or built, how much will it cost?
3. How much paid help will be needed; for example, interviewers, experimental confederates, coders?
4. If the analysis involves use of a computer, is machine time available without charge? If not, computer costs can mount astronomically.
5. Are any sources of funds available? (Scott and Wertheimer, 1962, pp. 22–23, have a very informative discussion of sources of financial support for research. Although it is focused primarily on research in psychology, much of the discussion is applicable to research in any of the social sciences.)

D. Cooperation from others

The discussion so far assumes that the procedures that are contemplated are feasible if enough time and money are available. But procedures that seem on their face to be quite feasible frequently turn out not to be. The problems are of two major kinds: those involved in dealing with other people, and those involved in using complex equipment.

Unless the study is to be carried out in an experimental laboratory, it is often necessary to get permission, if not active cooperation, from people in positions of authority in the settings to which the investigator needs access. This may be a delicate and difficult procedure, even if the proposed research operations involve little or no disruption of the ongoing activities in the setting. For example, in a study of the relationship between individual characteristics (personality traits, family background, and so on) and school achievement, the investigator may want to administer a questionnaire to students in the public schools. The questionnaire may take "only half an hour" to administer. To the investigator, the questions may seen quite innocuous. But some children talk at home about what has gone on at school during the day, especially if it involved any variation from the usual routine. And the school principal or superintendent is likely to remember the irate parent who telephoned to protest that the questionnaire item, "How often do you go to church?" was an intrusion into an area protected by the Bill of Rights, or that asking tenth graders "Are you ever preoccupied with thoughts about sex?" was pornographic —not to mention the parents and organizations that have, over the years, objected to any questions about the students' race or religion or their attitude toward other racial or religious groups. Against this background, many public school administrators have decided to simplify their lives by refusing permission for any outsider to carry out research of any sort within their school system. Beyond these concerns, there are the rights of freedom from invasions of privacy specified in ethics codes of the various social science disciplines (see Chapter 7).

If the proposal involves some modification of procedure within an ongoing institution, difficulties of a somewhat different sort are likely to arise. Suppose the investigator has the hypothesis that a different way of teaching reading might be more effective with children from disadvantaged backgrounds than the one now being used; or that in a compensatory program at the high school or college level, tutoring focused on methods of studying, test taking, and so on, would be more effective than tutoring focused on specific subject matter. Perhaps other investigators propose that training police, summoned in the course of violent family quarrels, in techniques of handling these quarrels as problems in human relations rather than in terms of criminal offenses would lead to a reduction in violent crimes arising out of such quarrels, and perhaps even to better relations between the police and the residents of the neighborhoods in which they work. All of these may be good ideas, and the people now supervising or actually carrying out the relevant activities may agree that they are worth trying. But most people do not like having their usual ways of doing things interfered with. For one thing, it is usually easier to keep on doing what one has been doing than to do it differently. For another, most people probably believe that the way they are doing whatever they are doing is reasonably effective; if they did not, they themselves might have tried doing it differently.

Suppose, however, that the relevant people within the institution—both administrators and operational staff—agree that some new program, or a variation of one already being carried on, would be worth trying on an experimental basis. With the best will in the world on all sides, difficulties arise. Who is to carry out the new program? If it is the investigator or someone else whose training and experience has been primarily in research and not in the particular setting chosen for this study, he or she will find that there will arise any number of problems and procedures not directly relevant to the research question. Moreover, the investigator's inexperience in dealing with them may jeopardize the whole research undertaking. Let us say that the investigator has taken the trouble to become an expert in the new technique of reading that is to be tried out; but how does the investigator handle disciplinary problems that may become so disruptive as to take the attention of the entire class away from the reading lesson? If one or more persons already on the staff are given the responsibility for carrying out the new program, what assurance is there that they will adhere to it in all necessary detail? They may not fully understand what they are expected to do. They may inadvertently slip back into habitual ways of doing things. Or it may turn out that they have strong preconceptions that one of the alternative ways being tried is much more likely to be effective than the other. A kind of ethical problem may then arise; it may seem to them unfair to subject one group to the treatment that they believe will be relatively ineffective, and so, consciously or not, they may not carry out that treatment.

An actual example may make this kind of problem clearer. A research group led by Deutsch and Collins (the same research group that carried out the housing study described earlier in this chapter) became interested in the question of whether feelings accompanying pleasant experiences with members of a different racial group in a particular setting might be generalized to attitudes toward other members of that group and other settings. Their own theoretical background, plus questions raised in an experience survey of group workers in interracial settings, led to a specific research problem: Given a recreation setting in which Black and white children frequently engage in group activities that they all enjoy, does calling attention to the interracial composition of the group increase the likelihood that the pleasurable feeling will become associated with the racial group label and thus lead to more favorable attitudes toward that group as a whole? The specific operation that was proposed was that, in such pleasant situations, some group leaders would make some such comment as "Here we all are, some of us Black and some white, all having fun together," whereas other leaders would refrain from any comment on the composition of the group. The research group approached the director of a community center, who was interested in the idea. It was discussed with the group work staff of the center, who also said they thought it was an interesting idea and worth trying. It was agreed that the two different approaches would be worked into the ongoing activities of the center by having half of the group leaders call attention to the interracial composition of the group at appropriate times when the youngsters were having fun, while the other half of the leaders would not. As far as possible, the leaders were matched in terms of their characteristics and those of their groups (for example, young men leading groups of ten- to twelve-year-olds); one member of each pair was designated to use the "calling attention" technique and the other not to. The groups were observed at specified intervals by members of the research staff. After a few weeks they realized that very little of the "calling attention" was going on in the groups that were supposed to be receiving that treatment, even though there were many opportunities for it. Further discussion with the group leaders revealed that, although in principle they had accepted the idea that this procedure was worth trying, they really believed it was undesirable to call attention to race under any circumstances, and so, consciously or not, those leaders who were supposed to use this procedure simply had not done so. And so there had been no experiment.

E. Availability of research subjects

Nor is it only the people whose help is needed in making arrangements or in carrying out experimental variations who may present difficulties. In any study that requires even minimal cooperation on the part of the people who are to be studied, one needs to consider whether subjects with the needed characteristics, under the planned conditions, are likely to be available and willing to take part in the research.

Does the plan of the study call for a mailed questionnaire? Returns of such questionnaires are notoriously low—from 10 to 40 percent—and it is almost certain that the individuals who respond differ from those who do not in ways that may significantly affect the findings. Does the design involve interviews with some specified sample of a population? Some people seem never to be at home when interviewers call; others, though at home, may refuse to open the door or to answer questions.

Some problems require as subjects only those people with specified characteristics, but people with such characteristics may be precisely the ones who are least willing to take part in research of the kind that is contemplated—or, for that matter, in any research. Studies of the effects of attitudes on one or another kind of behavior, for example, often require subjects with extreme attitudes on opposite sides of some controversial issue. But extreme attitudes at one end of some issues tend to be correlated with opposition to, or suspicion of, social science. Does the problem call for some subjects who are strongly in favor of racial integration and some who are equally strongly opposed? Does it require some subjects who think community mental health programs are a panacea for all sorts of social problems and others who think the "mental health movement" is a communist plot? Does it need some subjects who think sex education in the public school curriculum is urgently needed and others who see it as "introducing pornography"? People who think the "mental health movement" is part of a communist plot are likely to think social research is part of the same plot. Those who consider sex education pornographic are likely to react similarly to interviews on the subject.

Some members of minority groups may resent being "studied," feeling that what is needed is not research but action. Factory workers may perceive the researcher in an industrial setting as a confederate of "management," out to see how more work can be gotten out of them for less money. Many citizens of "developing countries" may suspect any researcher from the United States of being an agent for the Central Intelligence Agency, even though his interest may in fact be in some such problem as the effect of technological changes on family structure. In short, many individuals in some situations may be resentful, hostile, or suspicious of the investigator's motives. If the research plan calls for interviews with such individuals, or even for simple observation of their activities with their knowledge, the researcher may be in trouble.

F. Equipment

In other words, people sometimes introduce difficulties. Unfortunately, so does equipment. Much technical equipment, which sounds wonderfully precise when one reads about it, may be for the novice a major disappointment. Quite aside from the possibility that the equipment may break down, the kinds of data it yields may not be nearly so clear-cut as one would suppose. For example, measures of physiological reactions, such as galvanic skin response, vasomotor constriction, and pupil dilation, which are presumably beyond the subject's precise control, seem tempting. So too do measures based on perception under special circumstances, such as simultaneous presentation of different stimuli to the subject's right and left eyes. But an individual's physiological responses are highly unstable and easily influenced by conditions not relevant to the research problem but difficult to control, such as slight noises, the general arousal level of the subject, irregular breathing, and so on. And in perceptual studies, dominance of one or the other eye, and fluctuations in the degree of dominance, may obscure the effects of the variations in stimuli in which the researcher is interested.

G. Avoidance of trouble

How can such difficulties be foreseen? Obviously, not all of them can. But some of them are well-known to experienced investigators. An important step, then, is to check your plans with someone who has done, or is doing, research of the kind you contemplate. He or she may be able to steer you away from booby traps, or at least alert you to pitfalls of which you might otherwise have been unaware. Such a person may even be able to suggest alternative procedures that are more likely to be feasible.

Another precaution, especially in studies that are to be carried out in natural settings, is to explore all the possible sources of difficulty that you can think of, before you put a lot of work into the study. For example, if your research plan calls for administering a questionnaire in one or more schools, it is wise to check whether you can get permission from the school authorities to administer such a questionnaire, before you invest time in developing the questionnaire or pretesting it.

Another way of discovering possible problems while there is still time to remedy them is to carry out a small pilot study. You may discover that the technical equipment is not always reliable. You may find that the operations you were planning to use to induce your experimental conditions do not work for some subjects; for example, the film or the instructions you were planning to use to create a stress situation do not produce tension in some subjects. In investigating some problems, it is essential that the subjects not guess the purpose or "see through" the manipulations; for example, Asch (1958) would have been left without a study if any substantial number of subjects realized that their supposed fellow subjects were confederates of the experimenter who were giving rigged answers. If your study involves any deception, or even simply keeping subjects in ignorance of what you are interested in, it is a good idea to run a pilot study in which you check whether the subjects actually do suspect what you are up to—or, for that matter, whether they make some mistaken assumption which may also distort the results. In fact, you should consider the use of alternatives to deception. The prevailing expectation among captive subjects such as undergraduate students probably is that deception *is* involved in much social science research. This expectation, even if incorrect, can have a powerful effect upon research results.

H. Decision to abandon or revise

What does one do if he or she finds that it is not feasible to carry out a study as planned? One's first reaction is likely to be to drop the whole thing and start searching for a different problem. This may occasionally be the wisest course, but it is not usually so, and it should never be done without carefully considering the possibility of modifications that will make the project feasible. Suppose one's plan called for administering questionnaires to tenth graders in a public school, but it turns out that in the community where one had planned to do the study (usually selected simply because of geographical convenience) there is an inflexible rule against permitting research of any kind in the public schools. Are there neighboring communities where the public schools are more hospitable to research? Does the problem really require that the questionnaires be administered in or through the public schools, or was the school approach selected simply as a convenient way of getting teen-agers as subjects? If the latter, is it possible to reach teen-agers through recreation centers, church youth groups, Scouts, and similar organizations? Teen-agers who belong to such groups almost certainly differ from the general population of teen-agers in many characteristics, but these differences may or may not be important, depending on the particular problem to be studied.

Does the problem involve comparing two different treatments in a naturalistic setting? Ideally, the investigator would want to have a share in planning the treatments and in assigning subjects to them. The administrators may be willing to have the investigator observe, interview, or collect data in ways that do not interfere with ongoing activities, but may not be willing to modify procedures or to assign people to different conditions on the basis of the researcher's needs; in fact, there may be practical circumstances that make it impossible to do so. For example, in studying the effects of occupancy pattern in interracial housing projects, the ideal design would call for: housing projects within the same community differing in occupancy pattern, random assignment of applicants to one or the other pattern, and some measure of applicants' racial attitudes before they moved into the projects. None of these conditions was present in the interracial housing study described earlier in this chapter. In fact, the first two are not likely ever to occur; policies about occupancy pattern are usually community wide, and applicants cannot be transferred from one community to another simply for the sake of a research design. The third condition—measurement of attitudes before residence in the project —might be feasible if the timing of the study happened to coincide with the opening of a new project. But then, assuming that it takes some time for different occupancy patterns to have an impact on behavior and attitudes, the time lapse required would introduce problems of research budget and similar practical difficulties. Does one then conclude that it is hopeless to try to study the effects of different occupancy patterns? Deutsch and Collins did not. Recognizing that the possibilities available to them fell far short of an ideal research design, they nevertheless decided to take advantage of the existence of different patterns in neighboring cities, and, as far as possible, to build into their study checks on whether the departures from ideal research conditions were likely to have seriously affected their findings.

Sometimes a little reflection will make it clear that there is a situation right at hand, under your control, in which the variations whose effects you want to study can be introduced. Are you teaching a class—even one recitation section of an introductory lecture course? There are some problems that cannot effectively be studied in the classroom, but others for which it provides an ideal natural setting. For example, one of the variables in which Deutsch and Collins were interested was physical proximity; for their particular purpose, interracial housing projects provided the ideal setting. Festinger, Schachter, and Back (1950) also used housing projects as the setting for investigating the effects of physical proximity on the development of personal relationships. Other investigators have studied the effects of varying degrees of proximity in still larger communities on such variables as racial attitudes, development of social relationships, and even marriages. At the other extreme, Milgram (1965) varied the distance between subject and "victim" and between subject and experimenter as two of the influences in a highly controlled laboratory study of "destructive obedience," or the willingness to follow orders even at the cost of seriously injuring another person.

Are you interested in the effects of competitive versus cooperative conditions on performance? They can be (and have been) studied in real-life work situations, in elaborate field experiments, and in innumerable laboratory studies. But again, Deutsch (1949) took advantage of his position as an instructor to set up different arrangements for grading: some in which all members of a subgroup would receive the same grade, based on the joint product of the subgroup; others in which each individual's grade was based on his or her own work in comparison with that of others.

Suppose your problem involves a laboratory study in which you need experimental confederates (to give false answers, to give different instructions to subjects in different conditions, to be the supposed victims of electric shock). Sometimes fellow students are willing to perform these functions (usually with the understanding that they can call on you for similar help when they need it), but often the time required and the scheduling problems are so great that one cannot realistically count on volunteer help. On the other hand, paying confederates can become very expensive. Can you substitute tape recordings or written instructions without undermining your study?

Studies calling for elaborate and expensive equipment may be the most difficult to modify. Even here, however, it may sometimes be possible to work out a solution. If the problem is that the equipment is not available in the institution where you are planning to carry out the research and is too expensive for your budget, it pays to check whether such equipment is available at some other institution where you might be permitted to use it. One way of going about this is to write investigators who have been doing research with such equipment and ask if arrangements could be worked out for you to use it. If it becomes clear that you cannot get access to such equipment, or if it turns out that there are technical problems in its use that may take a long time to solve, it is a good idea to reconsider whether that equipment is really essential to your study. Let us say you were planning to measure pupil dilation as an indicator of the effect of the factors you were investigating, but the equipment for measuring pupil dilation turns out to involve complicated problems. Is pupil dilation really the focus of your research problem, or had you selected it simply as a presumably objective and sensitive indicator? If the latter, would it be possible to use cruder but simpler indicators, such as time spent looking at different stimuli, movements toward or away from them, or subjects' ratings of their responses?

VI. CONSIDERING THE ETHICS OF THE STUDY AS PLANNED

Questions of ethics in social science research have been raised with increasing frequency in recent years. The issues are complex and are discussed in detail in Chapter 7. However, some of the major considerations can be sketched briefly here; obviously, they should be considered before one settles on a research plan.

It goes without saying that investigators have a responsiblity not to damage the health or welfare of their subjects. The tricky questions involve how much damage or discomfort a given study may produce. For example, much research hinges on keeping subjects ignorant of the purpose of a study or deceiving them about its purpose. Is deception per se bad? Are there circumstances under which it is likely to be harmful, others where it is not? Many studies involve such matters as anxiety, stress, reaction to threat or danger; can such studies be carried out without at least temporary discomfort to the subjects? How severe is the discomfort likely to be, and how long lasting? Do the procedures involve unwarranted invasion of privacy? Is it reasonable to suppose that careful discussion with subjects after completion of the study can undo whatever discomfort may have been engendered?

If the contemplated procedures are likely to cause discomfort, loss of dignity, or invasion of privacy, is it possible to think of other, less drastic, ways of investigating the problem? If not, the investigator must consider carefully whether the potential contribution of the study to the general store of knowledge is great enough to outweigh the potential harm to subjects. If there is any question at all on this point, it is mandatory to discuss it with colleagues or advisers, who are likely to be more objective judges of the issue—and who may also be able to suggest precautions that can be taken to protect subjects while carrying out the study.

Ethical responsibilities of the researcher extend beyond treatment of the actual participants in the study. There is also a responsibility to the social groups represented by the subjects; it must be assured that unwarranted conclusions are not made about them. In the past, researchers have sometimes overgeneralized or misinterpreted their data, leading to well-publicized statements that make certain groups—certain racial or ethnic groups, certain ages, women—appear to be inferior. These "conclusions" are often used to establish governmental policy toward these groups. The set of ethical standards recently developed by the American Psychological Association is quite explicit about this; it states in Principle I(a) that researchers should: ". . . provide thorough discussion of the limitations of their data and alternative hypotheses, especially where their work touches on social policy or what might be construed to the detriment of specific age, sex, ethnic, socio-economic, or other social categories."

VII. SUMMARY

The choice of a general topic for research may arise from any source, including the researcher's own interests and values. Before it can serve as the basis for a study, however, it must be narrowed down into *a specific problem that can be investigated by scientific procedures.* In order to provide a guide for research, the concepts involved in the problem must be feasible to carry out the operations.

In the course of specifying the problem, one necessarily defines his or her concepts, decides on ways of translating them into operations, and perhaps formulates specific hypotheses. One also anticipates future steps: the kinds of subjects that are needed; how the data will be collected and analyzed; perhaps in a general way, the kind of report that will be written. Since all of these steps vary to some extent, depending on the type of problem, they are discussed in later chapters.

Three aspects, however, must be considered carefully in the course of formulating the problem: whether it is *feasible,* whether it is *ethical,* and how its findings will *relate to a larger body of knowledge.* If the proposed study is so broad in its scope as to be unmanageable within the time and money available, if it requires cooperation from other people which is not forthcoming, or if it calls for complicated equipment that is not available or that cannot be used without special training, much time and effort can be expended to no avail. Therefore it is important to think carefully in advance about the practical difficulties that may arise, and, if they seem likely to be serious, to consider whether the proposed study can be modified in ways that make it more likely to be workable without losing its point. Similarly, it is important to consider whether the study as planned may cause discomfort or damage to the subjects, and, if this seems likely, to consider whether the problem can be investigated by less drastic procedures. If it seems that it cannot be, the balance between the potential contribution of the study to the general store of knowledge and the potential harm to subjects must be carefully weighed.

One might think that the question of how the findings of the study relate to other knowledge can be postponed until, say, the time of writing the report. However, this is not so. Unless this question is considered at the very beginning, and kept in mind as the study is planned, one may end up finding that he or she has produced a study which may be interesting in its own right but which makes little or no contribution to the general body of scientific knowledge because the strings by which it could be tied to that body of knowledge—whether in the form of theory or of data—are missing.

chapter 4

RESEARCH DESIGN
EXPLORATORY AND DESCRIPTIVE STUDIES

Once the research problem has been formulated clearly enough to specify the types of information needed, investigators must work out their *research design*. A research design is the arrangement of conditions for collection and analysis of data in a manner that aims to combine relevance to the research purpose with economy in procedure. It follows that research designs will differ depending on the purpose of the research.

Each study, of course, has its own specific purpose. But we may think of research purposes as falling into a number of broad groupings: (1) to gain familiarity with a phenomenon or to achieve new insights into it, often in order to formulate a more precise research problem or to develop hypotheses; (2) to portray accurately the characteristics of a particular individual, situation, or group (with or without specific initial hypotheses about the nature of these characteristics); (3) to determine the frequency with which something occurs or with which it is associated with something else (usually, but not always, with a specific initial hypothesis); (4) to test a hypothesis of a causal relationship between variables.

In studies that have the first purpose listed above—generally called *formulative* or *exploratory* studies—the major emphasis is on discovery of ideas and insights. Therefore, the research design must be flexible enough to permit the consideration of many different aspects of a phenomenon.

exploratory studies

In studies having the second and third purposes listed above, a major consideration is accuracy. Therefore a design is needed that will minimize *bias* and maximize the *reliability* of the evidence collected. (*Bias* results from the collection of evidence in such a way that one alternative answer to a research question is favored. Evidence is *reliable* to the extent that we can assert confidently that similar findings would be obtained if the process of collecting the evidence was repeated. For a detailed discussion of bias and reliability in connection with measurement procedures, see Chapter 6.) Since studies with these second and third purposes present requirements for research design, we can treat them together; we shall call them *descriptive* studies.

descriptive studies

Studies testing *causal* hypotheses require procedures that will not only reduce bias and increase reliability but will permit inferences about causality. Experiments are especially suited to meeting this latter requirement. However, many studies concerned with testing hypotheses about causal relationships cannot be cast in the form of experiments.

In practice, these different types of study are not always sharply distinguishable. Any given research may have in it elements of two or more of the functions we have described as characterizing different types of study. In any single study, however, the primary emphasis is usually on only one of these functions, and the study can be thought of as falling into the category corresponding to its major function. In short, although the distinctions among the different types of study are not clear-cut, by and large they can be made; and, for the purpose of discussing appropriate research designs, it is useful to make them.

I. FORMULATIVE OR EXPLORATORY STUDIES

Many exploratory studies have the purpose of formulating a problem for more precise investigation or for developing hypotheses. An exploratory study may, however, have other functions: increasing investigators' familiarity with the phenomenon they wish to investigate in a subsequent, more highly structured study, or with the setting in which they plan to carry out such a study; clarifying concepts; establishing priorities for further research; gathering information about practical possibilities for carrying out research in real-life settings; providing a census of problems regarded as urgent by people working in a given field of social relations.

Our discussion will focus on studies that are directed primarily toward the formulation of problems for more precise investigation or toward the development of hypotheses. The points made and the procedures described are, however, applicable to exploratory studies having other goals.

The relative youth of social science and the scarcity of social science research make it inevitable that much of this research, for a time to come, will be of a pioneering character. Few well-trodden paths exist for the investigator of social relations to follow; theory is often either too general or too specific to provide clear guidance for empirical research. In these circumstances, exploratory research is necessary to obtain the experience that will be helpful in formulating relevant hypotheses for more definitive investigation.

Suppose, for example, that we are interested in obtaining insight into the process by which social environment influences psychological disorders. Although there has been much speculative writing on this topic and some research that is incidentally related to it, research workers entering this area are not in a position to advance any precise hypothesis for investigation. Indeed, it would be foolhardy for them to try to do so. Without some knowledge of the scope of the area, of the major social variables influencing psychological disorders, of the settings in which these variables occur, any hypothesis that is set forth is likely to be trivial. In the case of problems about which little knowledge is available, an exploratory study is usually most appropriate.

Occasionally there is a tendency to underestimate the importance of exploratory research and to regard only experimental work as "scientific." However, if experimental work is to have either theoretical or social value, it must be relevant to broader issues than those posed in the experiment. Such relevance can result only from adequate exploration of the dimensions of the problem with which the research is attempting to deal.

Although, for the most part, we are discussing the exploratory study as an entity, it is appropriate to consider it also as an initial step in a continuous research process. In practice, the most difficult portion of an inquiry is its initiation. The most careful methods during the later stages of an investigation are of little value if an incorrect or irrelevant start has been made. As Northrop (1947) has pointed out:

> Again and again investigators have plunged into a subject matter, sending out questionnaires, gathering a tremendous amount of data, even performing experiments, only to come out at the end wondering what it all proves. . . . Others, noting the success of a given scientific method in one field, have carried this method hastily and uncritically into their own, only to end later in a similar disillusionment. All such experiences are a sign that the initiation of inquiry has been glossed over too hastily, without any appreciation of its importance or its difficulty.

For whatever purpose an exploratory study is undertaken, ingenuity and good luck will inevitably play a part in determining its productiveness. Nevertheless, it is possible to suggest certain methods that are likely to be especially fruitful in the search for important variables and meaningful hypotheses. These methods include: (1) a review of the related social science and other pertinent literature; (2) a survey of people who have had practical experience with the problem to be studied; and (3) an analysis of "insight-stimulating" examples. Most exploratory studies utilize one or more of these approaches.

Whatever method is chosen, it must be used flexibly. As the initially vaguely defined problem is transformed into one with more precise meaning, frequent changes in the research procedure are necessary in order to provide for the gathering of data relevant to the emerging hypotheses.

A. A survey of the literature

One of the simplest ways of economizing effort in an inquiry is to review and build upon the work already done by others. In a study of the type we are discussing here, the focus of review is on hypotheses that may serve as leads for further investigation. Hypotheses may have been explicitly stated by previous workers; the task then is to gather the various hypotheses that have been put forward, to evaluate their usefulness as a basis for further research, and to consider whether they suggest new hypotheses. More frequently, however, an exploratory study is concerned with an area in which hypotheses have not yet been formulated; the task then is to review the available material with sensitivity to the hypotheses that may be derived from it.

In many areas a bibliographical survey will undoubtedly be more time consuming than rewarding; often one will find that no research of significance has been done in one's area of interest. This is perhaps less often true, however, than is assumed by those who fail to build upon the work of previous investigators. In any case, the conclusion that there is no relevant material would be unjustified without a thorough search of journals which are likely to carry articles on the given topic, and of such publications as the *Psychological Abstracts*, the *Child Development Abstracts and Bibliography*, the *Sociological Abstracts*, the listing of *Doctoral Dissertations Accepted by American Universities* compiled for the Association of Research Libraries, and the *Dissertation Abstracts* available in microfilm from University Microfilms, Ann Arbor, Michigan. In addition to these general sources, some government agencies and voluntary organizations publish listings or summaries of research in their special fields of interest. For example, the Children's Bureau of the U.S. Department of Health, Education, and Welfare publishes a bulletin of *Research Relating to Children;* the Anti-Defamation League of B'nai B'rith issues *Research Reports,* which are summaries of research relevant to intergroup relations. Professional organizations, research groups, and voluntary organizations are sources of information about unpublished research in their specific fields.

It would be a mistake to confine one's bibliographical survey to studies that are immediately relevant to one's area of interest. Perhaps the most fruitful means of developing hypotheses is the attempt to apply to the area in which one is working concepts and theories developed in completely different research contexts. Thus, the theory of adaptation level developed in work on psychophysical problems may provide stimulating analogies for work on factors influencing, for example, the perception of characteristics of members of an ethnic group other than one's own; level-of-aspiration theory may provide a parallel for studying changing community goals; learning theory may give insights into the process of attitudinal change; the concepts of "role," "political alienation," "social norm," "psychological need," "frustration," "group structure," and so on, may direct attention to important variables in any new situation to be studied.

The sensitive descriptions to be found in the works of creative writers are also a fertile ground of hypotheses for study. Although social scientists do not aim at capturing the richness of the novelist's descriptions, they may find in the world's literature many stimulating suggestions about important variables in the situations they wish to study. For example, Alan Paton's *Cry,* the *Beloved Country* and *Too Late the Phalarope*, Jean-Paul Sartre's *Portrait of the Anti-Semite*, Richard Wright's *Native Son*, and Eldridge Cleaver's *Soul on Ice* are laden with penetrating analyses of the causes and consequences of prejudice.

B. The experience survey[1]

Probably only a small proportion of existing knowledge and experience is ever put into written form. Many people, in the course of their everyday experiences, are in a position to observe the effects of alternative decisions and actions with respect to problems of human relations. The director of a settlement house and the group workers on its staff are likely to develop insights into the characteristics of young delinquents and the probable effectiveness of various approaches to them. The psychiatric social worker may acquire sensitivity to the environmental conditions that impede the adjustment of patients released from a mental institution and, on the other hand, to factors that support adjustment. The seasoned diplomat or overseas traveler may be well acquainted with the stages of adjustment any foreign sojourner goes through. Such specialists acquire, in the routine of their work, a reservoir of experience that could be of tremendous value in helping social scientists to become aware of the important influences operating in any situation they may be called upon to study. It is the purpose of an experience survey to gather and synthesize such experience.

The selection of respondents. Research economy dictates that the respondents in an experience survey be carefully selected. The aim of the experience survey is to obtain insight into the relationships between variables rather than to get an accurate picture of current practices or a simple consensus as to best practices. One is looking for provocative ideas and useful insights, not for the statistics of the profession. Thus the respondents must be chosen because of the likelihood that they will offer the contributions sought. In other words, a *selected* sample of people working in the area is called for.

In an experience survey it is a waste of time and effort to interview people who have little competence, or little relevant experience, or who lack ability to communicate their experience. An individual may have worked in a field for a number of years and not necessarily be a good informant. Perhaps the most direct method of selecting informants is to ask strategically placed administrators working in the area one desires to study to point out the most informative, experienced, and analytical people. Although this does not guarantee "insight-stimulating" respondents, one does obtain through this method people with a reputation for good experience

[1] Much of the following is based on an unpublished article by C. Selltiz, S. W. Cook, and R. Hogrefe entitled "The Experience Survey: A Step in Program Design for Field Research on Unexplored Problems."

and good ideas. The likelihood of their being useful informants is, of course, increased if they are recommended by more than one source, particularly if the different sources are known to have dissimilar points of view.

Although a random sample of practitioners may not be of value in an experience survey, it is nevertheless important to select respondents so as to ensure a representation of different types of experience. Wherever there is reason to believe that different vantage points may influence the content of observation, an effort must be made to include variation in point of view and in type of experience. Thus, for example, in an experience survey of factors affecting employee morale in industry, it is advantageous to interview representatives of both management and labor. It is also desirable to interview people at different levels in each group—workers, foremen, personnel managers, shop stewards, educational directors of unions, and so on—to obtain a varied perspective.

Apart from interviewing enough people to ensure adequate representation of different types of experience, there is no simple rule for determining the number of informants who should be interviewed in an experience survey. At a certain point, investigators will find that additional interviews do not provide new insights, that the answers fall into a pattern with which they are already familiar. At this point, further interviewing becomes less and less rewarding.

The questioning of respondents.   Before any systematic attempt is made to collect the insights of experienced practitioners, it is, of course, necessary to have some preliminary ideas of the important issues in the area. One source of such ideas, as we have previously indicated, is a bibliographical survey. Before an interview schedule for the systematic questioning of informants is developed, the information from such a survey almost invariably must be supplemented by a number of unstructured interviews[2] with people who have had extensive experience in the field to be investigated.

Even in the more systematic interviewing of the later informants, it is essential to maintain a considerable degree of flexibility. The purpose of providing the interview with structure is to ensure that all people interviewed respond to the questions the researcher wishes to have answered; however, the formulative and discovery functions of the experience survey require that the interview always allow the respondent to raise issues and questions the investigator has not previously considered.

In formulating questions for an interview schedule with social practitioners, it is generally useful to orient inquiries to "what works." That is, the questions should usually be of the following form: "If (a given effect) is desired, what influences or what methods will, in your experience, be most likely to produce it?" There are several reasons for focusing primarily

---

[2] For a discussion of "structured" and "unstructured" interviews, see Chapter 9.

on change-producing influences. First, social practitioners, necessarily heeding the imperatives of their work, are oriented toward producing change, toward "what works." They are more likely to understand and to be able to respond to a practically phrased question than to one that is worded abstractly. Second, the emphasis on change allows investigators to collect insights into processes operating over a period of time, which the practitioner is in a uniquely favorable position to observe. Third, if investigators' concerns are not only with the theoretical relationships among variables but also with their implications for social action, they need to know how these variables tend to cluster in everyday life and how these commonly found clusters of variables promote or hinder socially desirable objectives.

Where possible, in order to stimulate the informant to compare the major alternative methods for accomplishing a specific end, it is desirable to probe beyond a mere statement of general principles about producing a given change. Concrete illustrations, from the respondent's own experience, of successful and unsuccessful attempts to achieve a specific effect are of particular value. They enable investigators to collate experiences of different people in diverse circumstances and thus to form tentative conclusions and generalizations which go beyond the observations of any one informant.

To illustrate one type of question that has been found particularly useful in experience surveys, we present the following questions from such a survey of intergroup relations in industry.[3]

Some people believe that a non-discriminatory employment policy requires that minority group members with average qualifications for a particular job be brought into the job on a first-come-first-served basis. Other people believe that in introducing members of a minority group it is important for the first member of the group to have certain special qualifications. The assumption is that this will make it easier to get acceptance for other members of that minority group in this situation later.

Question: Should special qualifications be set for the first members of a minority group to be introduced into a new situation?

If the first members of a minority group introduced into a new situation are specially selected, there are several bases upon which the selection may be made.

Alternative A: Some people believe that the first members of a minority group introduced should be very high in ability for the particular job they are to fill.

Alternative B: Other people believe it is more important that the minority group members should be very pleasant and agreeable personally.

[3] This survey was conducted by J. Harding and R. Hogrefe of the Commission on Community Interrelations of the American Jewish Congress.

Alternative C: Still other people believe the main consideration is that the first minority group members be as similar as possible to the people they are to work with in physical appearance, manners, speech, education, interests, and previous experience.

Question: What are the relative advantages and disadvantages of these three principles for selecting the first members of a minority group to be introduced into a new situation?

In general, an experience-collecting interview is likely to be quite long, frequently lasting several hours. In view of the nature of the information wanted, it is desirable to prepare the respondent a week or so before the interview is to take place by sending a copy of the questions to be discussed. This gives the respondent an opportunity not only to do some advance thinking, but also to consult colleagues and to add the knowledge to be gained from their experiences.

Some by-products of experience surveys. An experience survey, as well as being a good source of hypotheses, can provide information about the practical possibilities for doing different types of research. Where can the facilities for research be obtained? Which factors can be controlled and which cannot in the situations one might wish to study? What variables tend to be clustered together in community settings? How ready are agencies, professional workers, and ordinary citizens to cooperate in controlled research studies of the problem in question? The answers to these and similar practical questions may be one of the by-products of a carefully planned experience survey. In addition, such a survey may provide a consensus of the problems considered urgent by the people working in a given area. This consensus may be extremely useful in establishing priorities in a program of research.

The report of an experience also provides a summary of the knowledge of skilled practitioners about the effectiveness of various methods and procedures in achieving specified goals. In lieu of more definitive knowledge, this information may be of enormous value as a guide to "best" practices in a given field. Of course, in presenting such a summary, it should be made clear that the survey was in no sense based on a random sample of workers in the field. Its usefulness comes from the presentation of insights and effective practices rather than from the presentation of the "typical."

C. The analysis of "insight-stimulating" examples[4]

Scientists working in relatively unformulated areas, where there is little experience to serve as a guide, have found the intensive study of selected

---

[4] Much of the following discussion is based on an unpublished paper by J. P. Dean, "The Method of Unstructured Pilot Inquiry." A condensation of this paper may be found in Dean (1954).

examples to be a particularly fruitful method for stimulating insights and suggesting hypotheses for research. The remarkable theoretical insights of Sigmund Freud were, of course, stimulated by his intensive studies of patients. So, too, profound changes in our conceptions of the relationship between human behavior and society have been brought about largely by anthropological studies of nontechnological cultures.

From these examples it should be clear that we are not describing what is sometimes called the "case-study" approach, in the narrow sense of studying the records kept by social agencies or psychotherapists, but rather the intensive study of selected instances of the phenomenon in which one is interested. The focus may be on individuals, on situations, on groups, on communities. The method of study *may* be the examination of existing records; it may also be unstructured interviewing or participant observation or some other approach.

What features of this approach make it an appropriate procedure for the evoking of insights? A major one is the *attitude* of the investigators, which is one of alert receptivity, of seeking rather than of testing. Instead of limiting themselves to the testing of existing hypotheses, they are guided by the features of the object being studied. Their inquiry is constantly in the process of reformulation and redirection as new information is obtained. Frequent changes are made in the types of data collected or in the criteria for case selection as emerging hypotheses require new information.

A second feature is the *intensity* of the study of the individual, group, community, culture, incident, or situation selected for investigation. One attempts to obtain sufficient information to characterize and explain both the unique features of the case being studied and those which it has in common with other cases. In the study of individuals, this may entail an extensive examination of both their present situation and their life histories. In the study of a group, an incident, and so on, individuals may be treated as informants about the object, rather than being themselves the objects of intensive analysis.

A third characteristic of· this approach is its reliance on the *integrative* powers of investigators, on their ability to draw together many diverse bits of information into a unified interpretation. This last characteristic has led many critics to view the analysis of insight-stimulating instances as a sort of projective technique, in which conclusions reflect primarily investigators' predispositions rather than the object of study. Even if this reproach is appropriate to many case studies, the characteristic is not necessarily undesirable when the purpose is to *evoke* rather than to *test* hypotheses. For even if the case material is merely the stimulus for the explicit statement of a previously unformulated hypothesis, it may serve a worthwhile function.

Social scientists who work with this approach have frequently found that the study of a few instances may produce a wealth of new insights, whereas a host of others will yield few new ideas. Although here, as elsewhere, no simple rules can be established for the selection of the instances to be studied, experience indicates that for particular problems certain types are more appropriate than others. We list below some of these types, together with the purposes for which they have been found most useful. The list is not exhaustive, nor are the types mutually exclusive.

1. The reactions of *strangers* or *newcomers* may point up characteristics of a community that might otherwise be overlooked by an investigator reared in the culture. A stranger is likely to be sensitive to social customs and practices that are more or less taken for granted by the members of a community. The resulting curiosity or surprise or bewilderment may call attention to features of community life to which members of the community have become so accustomed that they no longer notice them.

2. *Marginal individuals*, or groups, who are moving from one cultural grouping to another and are on the periphery of both groups, are similar in some respects to strangers or outsiders. Because they are "in between," exposed to conflicting pressures of the groups from and to which they are moving, they can often reveal dramatically the major influences operating in each group. For example, in the field of intergroup relations, the study of emigrants, of displaced persons, of Jews who are trying to be assimilated into local cultural groups, of women who are working in predominantly male occupations, of people who are in the process of conversion to or from Catholicism, or of people in areas of disputed national sovereignty, is likely to be highly rewarding.

3. Study of individuals or groups who are in *transition* from one stage of development to the next has been fruitful, particularly in anthropological investigations of the influence of culture upon personality. In carrying out an investigation of any culture, the anthropologist is necessarily limited by time to a cross-sectional study rather than one that would trace individuals from birth to death. The study of individuals who are at a point of transition helps overcome, to some extent, the limitations of a cross-sectional investigation. For example, intensive study of babies who are being weaned, or of adolescents, or of women in the period of menopause, is likely to give considerable insight into the process of change and into the socio-psychological characteristics of contiguous stages of development (see Mead, 1946). Similarly, the study of groups or societies in transition may be of value in understanding the processes of social change.

4. *Deviants, isolates,* and *pathological* cases may, by indirection, throw light on more common cases. The study of deviants (for example, individuals who are active in legislating for the decriminalization of possession of marijuana, although many of their associates hold traditional views) may serve to highlight the social norms and practices from which they are deviating (Becker, 1963). It may indicate the types of pressure to conform and the socio-psychological consequences of nonconformity; it may perhaps even help to reveal the methods by which social changes may be produced. In a similar manner, the analysis of isolates may accentuate the factors that produce cohesiveness in a given group or community. It may also reveal much about the way in which attitudes and information are transmitted in a social group (see, for example, Festinger, Schachter, and Back, 1950). The contributions of psychoanalysis to the understanding of personality are a striking illustration of the insights that may be uncovered by a

study of pathological cases, which frequently serve to underscore, through exaggeration, basic processes in nonpathological cases. Thus, for example, Ackerman and Jahoda (1950), in a study based on reports of psychoanalysts about cases under treatment, found that depressed patients are rarely prejudiced. This finding, with its implication that individuals who have turned their aggression against themselves do not need prejudice as a channel for aggression, provides an interesting hypothesis about the psychodynamics of prejudice. Extreme cases may also be enlightening when the interest is in social dynamics. The study of the breakdown of social controls and their reinstatement, as illustrated in natural disasters or a race riot—see, for example, Lee and Humphrey (1943)—may result in worthwhile insights into the processes of social control.

5. *Pure* cases are often productive. For example, Levy (1943) in his study of maternal overprotection, was interested in three questions: What leads a mother to be overprotective, what effects does maternal overprotection have on the child, and how can the difficulties that may result from overprotection be prevented or remedied? Reasoning that he could best find clues through the study of cases of *marked* overprotection, he examined many records of cases treated in a child guidance clinic. There were two major criteria for selecting cases for intensive study. First, they must show the mother's extreme overprotection, as evidenced by inseparability of mother and child, the mother's treating the child as a baby, and the mother's prevention of independent behavior on the part of the child. Second, they must be "pure" cases, in the sense that the mother's behavior was consistently overprotective and also in the sense that there was no evidence of rejection of the child. (This latter criterion was introduced on the ground that the combination of overprotection and rejection differs from overprotection per se and may have different origins and consequences.) Of the cases that met these criteria, only those were retained that contained enough information about the mother to make possible some inferences about the factors producing overprotective behavior, enough information about the child to yield insight into the kinds of problems produced by such behavior, and enough information about treatment of the case to give clues as to the effects of therapy. Of the more than five hundred cases examined, only twenty met all these criteria; these formed the basis of Levy's study.

6. The characteristics of individuals *who fit well* in a given situation and those *who do not fit well* provide valuable clues about the nature of the situation. Thus the knowledge that the people who feel at home in a given community, who seem to fit best, are either highly dependent or authoritarian in personality provides some insight into the characteristics of the community. Similarly, the discovery that those who feel thwarted by a given situation are the young and ambitious and those who have considerable personal initiative would provide a clue to the nature of the situation.

7. Selection of individuals who represent *different positions in the social structure* helps to produce a rounded view of the situation they are reflecting. In almost all social groups, one finds variations in social status and specialization of social roles or functions. Individuals occupying these different positions are likely to see any given situation from different perspectives, and this diversity is a source of insights. Thus, interviewing the janitors in a housing project may be as important for understanding relations within the project as interviewing the

manager. The discrepancies as well as the similarities in the social perceptions of people holding different positions or fulfilling diverse functions are frequently revealing.

8. A review of *investigators' own experiences* and a careful examination of their reactions as they attempt to "project" themselves into the situation of the subjects they are studying may be a valuable source of insights. After all, the "cases" with which investigators are likely to have the greatest familiarity (though also the most bias) are themselves. As Jones's biography (1953) of Freud makes clear, many of Freud's most valuable insights came from his efforts to understand himself. To be sure, there probably are few persons with the qualities of a Freud; we cannot expect that analysis of one's own experience will often have such fruitful results. But, even so, here is a source of ideas that ought not to be neglected. That the point needs to be made at all stems from the fact that scientists are often so preoccupied with the importance of objectivity that they actively strive to maintain as great a distance as they can between themselves and the objects of their study. In the stages of research in which one is looking for *ideas* rather than *conclusions*, such objectivity may be inappropriate.

Our listing of "insight-stimulating" cases is inevitably incomplete. The type of cases that will be of most value depends largely, of course, on the problem with which one is concerned. Nevertheless, it is generally true that in an exploratory study, cases that provide sharp contrasts or have striking features are most useful, since in exploratory work the discernment of minute differences is likely to be difficult.

It is important to remember that exploratory studies merely lead to insights or hypotheses; they do not test or demonstrate them. In selecting cases that have special characteristics, one has by definition chosen cases that are not typical. Although marginal, deviant, or pure cases are likely to be fruitful sources of ideas about processes that may occur in more typical cases, one cannot assume that these processes do in fact occur in cases other than those one has studied. Pressures on marginal individuals may be quite different from those on individuals who are well integrated in a group; deviant cases may be deviant not only in their behavior but in the psychological processes underlying the behavior. An exploratory study must always be regarded as simply a first step; more carefully controlled studies are needed to test whether the hypotheses that emerge have general applicability.

II. DESCRIPTIVE STUDIES

An enormous amount of social research has been concerned with describing the characteristics of communities. One may study the people of a community: their age distribution, their national or racial background, the state of their physical or mental health, the amount of education they have had—the list could be extended indefinitely. One may study community facilities and their use: the condition of housing, the extent to which libraries are used, the amount of crime in various neighborhoods—again, the list is endless. One may undertake to describe the structure of social organization in the community or the major patterns of behavior.

Another vast body of research has been concerned with estimating the proportion of people in a specified population who hold certain views or attitudes or who behave in certain ways: How many favor abortion as a method of birth control? How many believe that there will be a nuclear war? How many think capital punishment should be abolished? How many watched which television programs last week?

Still other studies are concerned with specific predictions: How many people will vote for a certain candidate? How many will purchase a new car during a given period? In what neighborhoods is the change in population likely to require building new schools or closing existing ones within the near future?

Others are concerned with discovering, or testing, whether certain variables are associated: Do more Catholics than Protestants vote Democratic? Do people who spend a good deal of time reading go to the movies often? Do girls, on the whole, learn to talk at an earlier age than boys? Note that none of these questions, as they have been presented, involves a hypothesis that one of the variables *leads to* or *produces* the other; questions embodying such hypotheses pose different requirements for research procedures.

This is a considerable array of research interests, which we have grouped under the heading of *descriptive* studies. We have grouped them together because, from the point of view of research procedures, they share certain important characteristics. The research questions presuppose much prior knowledge of the problem to be investigated, as contrasted with the questions that form the basis for exploratory studies. Investigators must be able to define clearly what it is they want to measure and must find adequate methods for measuring it. In addition, they must be able to specify who is to be included in the definition of "a given community" or "a given population." In collecting evidence for a study of this sort, what is needed is not so much flexibility as a clear formulation of *what* and *who* is to be measured and techniques for valid and reliable measurements.[5]

Descriptive studies are not limited to any one method of data collection. They may employ any or all of the methods to be presented in subsequent chapters. Thus, in a study of what befalls foreign sojourners as they learn to live abroad, Kidder (1971) used open-ended interviews, structured scales, and participant observation.

Although descriptive studies may use a wide range of techniques, this does not mean that they are characterized by the flexibility that marks exploratory studies. The procedures to be used in a descriptive study must be carefully planned. Because the aim is to obtain complete and accurate

[5] For a discussion of validity and reliability of measurement, see Chapter 6.

information, the research design must make much more provision for protection against bias than is required in exploratory studies. Because of the amount of work frequently involved in descriptive studies, concern with economy of research effort is extremely important. These considerations of economy and protection against bias enter at every stage: formulating the objectives of the study; designing the methods of data collection; selecting the sample; collecting, processing, and analyzing the data; and reporting the findings. The following paragraphs point out some of the ways in which economy and protection against bias are taken into account in the design of a descriptive study.[6] As an illustration, we shall consider a study of the experiences and attitudes of United States and European visitors to India (Kidder, 1971).

A. Formulating the objectives of the study

The first step in a descriptive study, as in any other, is to define the question that is to be answered. Unless the objectives are specified with sufficient precision to ensure that the data collected are relevant to the question raised, the study may not provide the desired information.

In our example, the general research question was: What changes occur in sojourners as they pass the time abroad? Much of the research on social relations has concerned the changes in attitudes of two or more groups who share the same nationality or live in the same city. Such studies have looked at shifts in racial attitudes as a result of changes in housing or school policies. If we think of these as studies of "domestic" social relations, an interesting question is: Do the same kinds of changes and social processes occur among persons who cross international boundaries? Do they become more or less tolerant of and favorable toward the people and customs of other nations?

In answer to the above question, a number of previous studies of international visitors yielded all possible answers: yes, no, and maybe. Some research reported an improvement in the social relations and attitudes of sojourners; other studies found a steady decline in foreigners' evaluations of the host country, and yet others reported a U-shaped curve with positive attitudes at the beginning and end of international journeys and a temporary depression in the middle. Such a tantalizing array of results might tempt a person to ask, "What is going on?" in such cross-cultural visits, and it is precisely such a question that leads to a descriptive study.

The object of the study described below was to follow the course of adjustment of foreign visitors in India by observing and interviewing persons who had been there for varying lengths of time to see how their views of themselves and of India changed.

[6] For a more detailed discussion of descriptive studies, and especially those that take the form of surveys of opinion, attitudes, and so on, see Hyman (1955, Part II) and Parten (1950).

B. Designing the methods of data collection

After the problem has been formulated specifically enough to indicate what data are required, the methods by which the data are to be obtained must be selected. Techniques for collecting the information must be devised if, as is likely, no suitable ones already exist. Each of the various methods—observation, interviewing, questionnaires, projective techniques, examination of records, and so forth—has its advantages and limitations, which are discussed in detail in later chapters.

As the reader will discover in the remainder of this book, there is a tremendous array of research methods from which to choose, and a person embarked on a maiden voyage hardly knows where to begin. Some seasoned researchers have their preferred approaches and their students may follow suit. Thus, some trust only controlled experiments and steer clear of surveys. Others feel comfortable only with participant observation and do not trust contrived experiments. Yet others feel that large sample surveys approximate the truth better than either of the above. For someone willing to contemplate any or all of these methods, the choice often is made by the practicalities of the situation, the nature of the research question, or the skills available to the researcher. Ultimately, social science would benefit if each research question was answered with data obtained from each of the above methods—for this would eliminate each method's peculiar weaknesses (see Campbell and Fiske, 1959). Generally, however, we are pressured by time and practical constraints to choose one method, leaving the rest for another day.

Once the general method of approach has been selected, other decisions remain to be made. Having decided, for instance, to survey a sample of the foreign residents in an Indian city, an investigator is left with the possibility of using a mail questionnaire or personal interview; and having decided on a mail questionnaire, should it contain forced-choice attitude scales or open-ended questions? Fortunately, not all of these are either-or issues, and we would in fact be best off using *both* structured attitude scales and open-ended questions on a questionnaire or interview schedule. Descriptive studies in particular benefit from choosing a variety of research formats to maximize their chances of capturing fully the social processes in any particular setting.

The study of foreign visitors in India did just that. It employed participant observation, open-ended interviews, and structured questions and attitude scales. The principal researcher was a participant in the foreign experience, being a United States citizen in India. As such she had automatic access to the group under investigation and did not have to work at gaining entry. As the reader will see in Chapter 8, however, other problems beset the observer after entry is secured—each investigator brings his or her own idiosyncratic set of biases and preconceived notions to the study, and these affect the accuracy of the observations. Thus, a person from the United States would probably record events differently from a Britisher in India, for they have different colonial histories in that land. Not only might their interpretations of a single event differ, but their very *selection* of what they observe and record may likely differ. The North American researcher of this study was sensitive to other United States citizens' attempts to "fit in" or blend into India—and that may be a peculiarly United States preoccupation.

If participant observation is heir to such errors of interpretation, one may argue that structured interviews and standardized attitude scales would provide a healthy complement and control for such subjective elements. **structured** Structured scales like the semantic differential discussed in Chapter 12 **scales** produce data which are almost totally uncontaminated by the investigator's views. For instance, few people would quarrel with the interpretation of the answer marked *X* in figure 4.1.

I would characterize most Indians as:

FIGURE 4.1   Example of a structured attitude scale.

In contrast to someone who checked the term "Dishonest," the respondent whose answer is shown above has a very favorable attitude toward his or her hosts.

In between the free form of observational methods and the rigid structure of attitude scales lie free-response questionnaire and interview items which ask standardized questions but permit wide ranging answers. Questions such as, "What five pieces of advice would you give a newcomer to India which would ease that person's adjustment?" elicit a rich array of responses.

Where possible, it is desirable to employ more than one method of gathering data—a judicious mixture of direct observation, free-response questions, and structured scales is almost guaranteed to provide a more thorough description of processes occurring in social relations than any of these alone.

C. Selecting the sample

In many—though by no means all—descriptive studies, investigators want to be able to make statements about some defined group of people or objects (in our example, sojourners). It is rarely necessary to study all the people in the group in order to provide an accurate and reliable description of the attitudes and behavior of its members. More often than not, a sample of the population to be studied is sufficient.

Much work has been done on the problem of designing samples in such a way that they yield accurate information with a minimum amount of research effort. At this point, it may be profitable to illustrate how an awareness of statistical considerations may result in considerable research economy. Rowntree (1941), in his classic study of poverty in York, England, investigated every working-class household. To check the accuracy of sampling methods, he selected, according to a systematic procedure, every tenth interview schedule and compared the results obtained thereby with those obtained from all the cases. Similar calculations were based on samples of one in twenty, one in thirty, one in forty, and one in fifty. Table 4.1 shows his results for one type of information—the proportion of income spent on rent by families in five different income groupings. It is apparent that the various samples, regardless of their size, gave results fairly close to those found for all the households in each income class. Thus, comparing the extreme right-hand column (figures based on a sample of one in fifty families) with the left-hand column (figures based on the complete survey), we see that the sample shows families in income class "A" spent 27.1 percent of their income on rent, while the total survey shows that such families spent 26.5 percent of their income on rent; in income class "B," the sample shows 22.6 percent of income spent on rent, while the total survey shows 22.7 percent; and so on. For no income group does the figure shown by the sample based on one family in fifty differ by more than 2 percentage points from that shown by the complete survey. In other words, essentially the same results would have been obtained by taking a sample of one in fifty instead of every working-class household in the city. That is, a substantial saving in time and effort could have been effected without significantly impairing the results.

Even very slight differences between figures—for example, the difference between 26.5 percent and 27.1 percent—may be statistically significant. In deciding whether a difference is worthy of attention, two kinds of considerations are relevant: statistical ones and practical ones. Whether a difference between two figures is *statistically significant* involves precisely the ques-

TABLE 4.1   **Percentage of Income Spent on Rent**[a]

Income Class	Complete Survey	Sample Surveys				
		1 IN 10	1 IN 20	1 IN 30	1 IN 40	1 IN 50
"A"	26.5	26.6	25.9	27.0	28.3	27.1
"B'	22.7	22.9	23.5	23.3	22.3	22.6
"C"	19.8	18.1	17.2	18.3	17.2	18.0
"D"	15.8	16.0	14.4	15.8	17.1	16.9
"E"	11.3	11.0	10.1	10.7	11.2	11.5

[a] From Rowntree (1941).

tion being discussed here—the probable deviation of figures based on samples from those for the total population from which the samples are drawn. If a particular difference is statistically significant, the decision whether it has practical significance is, of course, a matter for judgment in terms of the consequences of the different figures. If some major decision—as, for example, a general increase in wages—is to be made on the basis of the findings, then a difference of as little as 1 percentage point between the sample findings and the true state of affairs for the total population may be serious. However, in most surveys it seems unlikely that a difference as small as those shown in table 4.1 would lead to any major change in interpretation or in recommendations for action, if such recommendations were among the goals of the study.

It is, of course, important that the study findings based on a sample (that is, on only part of the group about which statements are to be made) should be a reasonably accurate representation of the state of affairs in the **population** total group (referred to, in sampling terminology, as the "population"). This means that the sample should be selected in such a way that findings based on it are likely to correspond closely to those that would be obtained if the population were studied. To bring this about, considerable attention has been paid to problems and methods of sampling.

When the population of persons or objects of a study is vast, it is essential to sample from this pool. When the population itself is small, an investigator may try to study the entire group, but even in such instances only a sample may respond. For instance, in a study of the effects of forced inter-racial rooming in college dormitories, Markley (1968) sent a mail survey to all of the sophomores in two colleges who had been assigned a roommate of a different race (that is, white or Black) during their freshman year. When the questionnaires were returned, the investigator ended up with less than the total population—only 54 percent of the group replied, and we can safely assume that this sample was in no sense randomly selected. The self-selection of respondents could have threatened the validity of any conclusions the investigator wished to draw; but a control group of students (white students who had white roommates) to whom the same questionnaire was sent produced a similar return rate, which would make it seem that the same process of selection or attrition was operating in both groups.

Occasionally, when the entire population of interest is a captive audience, a study may succeed in reaching and describing the entire group. Students in classrooms often have no effective choice of whether or not to be subjects in a study, particularly if the study is an observational or unobtrusive one. Often, however, one finds attrition from one cause or another, whether one aims for a systematically or randomly selected sample or the entire population. The missing persons may be ill, inaccessible, unwilling, unable, or in any other way indisposed. For instance, although Kidder (1971) tried to contact all of the known United States families living in a particular Indian city, some were never included because they were vacationing back in their homeland, a few could never find time to be interviewed, and one or two undoubtedly slipped into and out of that city without their names ever appearing on the list which the United States Information Service kept. Professional survey research organizations have a variety of search and call-back procedures like those of census takers to ferret out missing persons. Most descriptive research in social relations has neither the available staff nor the technology to obtain such 100 percent response rates, and the possible biases must consequently be examined.

The research purpose determines the appropriate sampling unit. In an election study, the sampling units would be eligible voters; in a study of family budgets, they would be families; in a study of infant behavior, they might be time periods. Whatever the sampling unit, it is important to have a basis for identifying the total population of such units and a specified method of selecting units from that population.

D. Collecting and checking the data

To obtain consistent data free from the errors introduced by individual interviewers, observers, and others, it is necessary to supervise the staff of field workers closely as they collect and record information. Checks must be set up, for example, to ensure that interviewers are honest and that the data they collect are unbiased.[7] As data are collected, they should be examined for completeness, comprehensibility, consistency, and reliability.

In the study of foreign sojourners, the interviews were conducted by two women from the United States. One indication that the answers received were relatively candid came from a comparison of a few interviews conducted by an Indian woman during the pretesting phase of the study. Both the Indian interviewer and the foreign respondents found those sessions difficult and embarrassing and tended to gloss over the questions and answers which would reflect negatively on either the host country or the visitors. In contrast to this, the North American interviewers obtained rather candid reports of incidents or experiences which could put either India or its guests in a bad light.

Just as in everyday life we assume that those people who make unpopular or risky statements are probably saying what they really believe, so also in social research we take socially undesirable or punishable responses as indexes of candor.

An excellent example of such reliability checking appears in a descriptive study of heroin addicts (Sanders, 1973). A potentially incriminating question, "Have you ever sold dope?" was included in the interviews with 160 addicts. When 61 percent of the addicts admitted to having sold heroin,

---

[7] For a discussion of "cheating" by interviewers and methods of defecting it, see Blankenship, *et al.* (1947).

the interviewers concluded: ". . . if a large group of known heroin addicts is willing to truthfully answer the most incriminating of questions at a rate considered to be reasonable, then it is . . . a fair assumption . . . that the remainder of the questions were answered in a relatively honest fashion" (Sanders, 1973, p. 31).

In addition to looking for socially dangerous or undesirable answers within the interview, Sanders employed several other procedures to maximize the reliability of his data. He employed four interviewers who were ex-addicts themselves and were working in the drug treatment program; and all four interviewers were Black, as were the respondents. Sanders also conducted training sessions in which he discussed the purposes of the research, the nature of the questionnaires, and techniques of interviewing. The interviewers were well equipped to understand the life and the language of an addict. They did not represent an outside establishment and could not be conned. And perhaps most important, they offered their respondents confidentiality, courtesy, and respect, in return for which they received what they judged to be a good deal of cooperation. Of the 169 addicts whom they wished to interview, only nine refused or gave apparently evasive answers.

E. Analyzing the results

The process of analysis includes: coding the interview replies or observations (placing each item in the appropriate category); tabulating the data (counting the number of items in each category); and performing statistical computations. These procedures are discussed in considerable detail in Chapter 14. Here we may simply note that both considerations of economy and the need for safeguards against error enter into each of these steps. In general, considerations of economy require that the analysis be planned in detail before actual work on it is started. In this way, investigators may avoid unnecessary labor, such as working out tables for which they later find they have no use or, on the other hand, redoing some tables because they failed to include relevant data. To be sure, complete planning of the analysis in advance is not always possible or even desirable; new ideas occur to investigators as they examine their preliminary findings. But, except in exploratory studies, it is always possible and desirable to work out in advance the basic outlines of the analysis.

Safeguards against error in coding ordinarily take the form of checking the reliability of the coders—that is, determining the extent to which they agree in assigning a given item to a given category. If the code requires complex judgments, the usual procedure is to have two or more coders independently code a sample of the material, continuing—with additional training or, if necessary, modifications in the code—until they have achieved a satisfactory degree of reliability. In the case of simple codes, one coder may process the entire group of cases without advance determination of reliability; a second person may then code, say, every twentieth case, in order to provide a check on accuracy.

If the material is to be tabulated by machine, it must be entered on appropriate cards; this is usually done by punching holes corresponding to a given code. It is advisable to check the accuracy of punching; again, it is usual to check at least a sample of the cards.

The accuracy of tabulation may also be checked by having a sample of the tables redone. However, at this stage it is possible to make a rough check by comparing figures from different tables. For example, the figures in each table should add up to the total number of cases, unless there is reason to omit some from a given table. Moreover, certain classifications are likely to be used in more than one table, and these figures provide a partial check on accuracy.

Finally, statistical computations are needed in a study of any complexity; averages, percentages, correlations must be computed. Again, these operations may be checked by having a second person redo a sample of them.

Statistical operations of another sort are introduced for the purpose of safeguarding against drawing unjustified conclusions from the findings. These involve such procedures as estimating from the sample findings the probable occurrence of some characteristic in the population the sample is intended to represent, and estimating the probability that differences found between subgroups in the sample represent differences between the corresponding subgroups in the population rather than simple chance differences due to sampling. (The logic underlying such procedures is discussed briefly in Chapter 14; the procedures are discussed in detail in standard statistics texts.)

sampling

The process of analysis in the study of foreigners in India ranged from straightforward assigning of numerical values to the structured attitude scales (such as, "I would describe most Indians as honest") to the subjective determination of whether advice to "avoid raw vegetables" reflected a positive or negative attitude toward India. The structured scales could be scored by anyone equipped with a simple instruction sheet. The wide ranging answers to the open-ended interview questions, however, required an elaborate code sheet and often lengthy deliberations before they could be assigned to a category. While structured scales often force the *respondent* to wonder what is meant by a particular question and its response alternatives, open-ended interviews require the *interviewer* or the *coder* to discern what is meant by particular answers. In response to a question which asked foreigners to imagine what advice they would give to a newcomer in India, the interviewers received over one hundred different answers, which at first glance seemed to represent over one hundred different opinions. After closer scrutiny, however, the researcher was able to discern some meaningful categories into which all of the answers could be placed. The three categories which emerged were: (1) approach India—

learn the customs, develop a taste for the food, venture forth without fear; (2) be cautious but considerate—practice tolerance and patience and be discreet in dress and demeanor; (3) avoid India—guard your money and your sanity. While some answers easily fit one of these categories, others seemed to fall somewhere in between. To handle such ambiguity, two researchers coded all of the answers independently of each other, and the analyses were performed separately on the data from each coder. The high rate of agreement between the results of these two coders gave evidence of the reliability of their subjective judgments.

The data obtained through participant observation were analyzed by one person—the observer. After rereading the two hundred pages of field notes several times, the investigator wrote down instances of events, comments, and attitudes which appeared often enough to merit counting. These instances were then examined again to see what themes stood out which would tell the story of sojourning in India.

The results of this study confirmed the multiple trends found in earlier work. On the one hand, sojourners became more aware of their being alien and more encapsulated in foreign enclaves the longer they lived abroad; they became socialized into a world consisting largely of other foreigners like themselves. On the other hand, they made more positive statements about India and would send more favorable impressions back home, the closer they came to leaving, perhaps in anticipation of the queries and misguided assumptions about India which they would encounter back home.

Without the structured scales and interview questions, we might question the reliability and objectivity of such research; and without the participant observation we would miss the richness and detail of the sojourners' lives. These methods and their results complement each other nicely.

III. PROBLEMS OF PERSPECTIVE

If we examine the interpersonal relations between a quarreling couple, we quickly realize that there are two sides to the story. Any examination of the social relations between two or more groups similarly encounters multiple perspectives but often chooses to consider only one. For instance, the study of foreigners in India described above was done from the point of view of the visitor and not that of the Indian host. Many studies of race relations in the United States are done from the point of view of the white person, rather than the Black, Mexican, or native American. Sometimes one-sided research results from a failure even to concede that there is another side. Sometimes it represents a conscious decision to examine one perspective alone. And sometimes it reflects the practical constraints on investigators.

The study of the effects of interracial rooming in college dormitories illustrates this problem (Markley, 1968; Markley and Osborn, 1972). The investigators sent mail questionnaires to Black students and white students who had been paired as roommates and to a control group of white students who had not had Black roommates their freshman year. When the data analyses were planned, it became obvious that the effects of interracial rooming on white students could be examined by comparing them with their control group; but for the Black students no such comparison could be made—none had been paired with Black roommates. This built-in bias reflected the policies and assumptions of those colleges and that era. Comparison of the two white groups revealed that interracial rooming was a positive learning experience for those students and led them to acquire their Black roommates' attitudes favoring Black self-determination. Fortunately, the questionnaires included questions which called for free responses, and some of the Black students drew their own comparisons. One student wrote: "I already know all I need about white persons, and I didn't learn all that much that was new. I resent having to be an unpaid teacher when I need to be spending my time with other Black students on our own concerns" (Markley and Osborn, 1972, p. 21). This suggests that while the experience was educational for one of the groups, it may have been only burdensome for the other; an outcome which underlines the existence of divergent perspectives.

Since there will inevitably be two or more sides to any story of social relations, various social scientists have urged that we make our values explicit (Sawyer, 1970), indicate whose side we are on (Becker, 1967), and enlist participation from as many diverse partners as possible in our research on social groups (Kidder and Stewart, 1975).

IV. SUMMARY

In this chapter we have pointed out that the function of research design is to provide for the collection of relevant evidence with minimal expenditure of effort, time, and money. These considerations are important in any study, whatever its purpose. But how they can best be achieved depends to a considerable extent on the research purpose. When the purpose of a study is exploration, a flexible research design, which provides opportunity for considering many different aspects of a problem, is appropriate. When the purpose of a study is accurate description of a situation or of an association between variables, accuracy becomes a major consideration; methods are needed that minimize bias and maximize the reliability of the evidence collected. Methods appropriate to exploratory and descriptive studies have been discussed in this chapter.

When the purpose of a study is to test a hypothesis of a cause-and-effect relation between variables, other requirements are introduced. Research designs appropriate for such studies are discussed in the following chapter.

chapter 5

METHODS FOR DETERMINING "CAUSAL" RELATIONSHIPS AMONG VARIABLES

A hypothesis of a causal relationship asserts that a particular characteristic or occurrence (X) is one of the factors that determine another characteristic or occurrence (Y). Studies designed to test such hypotheses must provide data from which one can legitimately infer that X does or does not enter into the determination of Y. It is important to understand clearly what we mean when we speak of a "causal relationship" among two or more variables. To say that X "causes" Y is merely to say that whenever X occurs, there is a likelihood that Y will follow at some later time. We observe concomitant variation between instances of X and instances of Y, and we have some theoretical reasons for believing that Y follows X in time. Nothing more should be read into the use of the term "cause." Cause does not imply, for instance, mysterious "forcings," "impulsions," or "ultimate goals that may draw people to them."

causal relationship

Popular use of the term "cause" often implies a billiard-ball-like sequence of events, as if *real* causes operate in a necessary and sufficient manner. There is, however, a broader conception in which contributory or partial causation is recognized and which views events in a probabilistic way. In social science, it is very difficult to think of factors that are both necessary and sufficient for the production of an effect. Even in the causation of disease, it is recognized that no agent automatically and uniformly causes illness. At best, we seek to identify sets of conditions, which, when taken together, are usually sufficient to produce an effect.

Causes, like stories, are not discovered; they are invented. A causal sequence is a perspective we place on the world. It is proper, then, to speak of a causal hypothesis and develop criteria for testing the adequacy of the formulation.

The general strategy that we employ in scrutinizing evidence for causal hypotheses is congenial with the strategies that are used in assessing evidence for any other kind of hypothesis, except that, on occasion, we attempt to garner evidence that bears on temporal ordering of variables. The strategy that we will outline in the rest of this chapter is one of *eliminating alternative explanations for the events that are under study.* If we cannot explain an event better by using plausible alternatives to that explanation encompassed in the hypotheses we are testing, it is necessary to be sensitive to two considerations: (1) the extent to which operations that we perform on the variables in our study are in fact producing the results that we think them to be (we shall discuss "the validity problem" in Chapter 6); (2) the extent to which we can generalize the findings in our studies to the social world beyond the particular study being done, whether experiment or survey. (The problem of sampling and "external validity" is also discussed more fully in Chapter 6.)

To summarize, the criteria for inferring causality include:

1. Covariation between the presumed cause and presumed effect
2. Proper time order, with the cause preceding the effect
3. Elimination of plausible alternative explanations for the observed relationship

Before we consider research procedures that can provide grounds for inferences of this sort, it may be helpful to consider some illustrations of problems we face in interpreting relationships among variables. For this purpose we shall consider some of the research on the relation between personal contact with members of a different racial group and attitudes toward the group.

I. PROBLEMS IN INTERPRETING RELATIONSHIPS AMONG VARIABLES: SOME EXAMPLES

The relation between intergroup contact and intergroup attitudes received a good deal of attention from social scientists in the 1940s and 1950s with some work continuing into the 1960s and the 1970s. In the 1940s there were a number of studies in which members of the majority group (usually college students) filled out questionnaires about the amount and kinds of contact they had had with members of specified minority groups (usually Jews and/or Blacks) and about their attitudes toward those groups (for example, Allport and Kramer, 1946; Harlan, 1942; MacKenzie, 1948). Most of these studies were concerned with the hypothesis that personal contact with members of a minority group leads to more favorable attitudes toward that group. However, while most studies found that a high degree of contact, under certain conditions, was associated with favorable attitudes, there was no evidence as to which had come first. Did people with initially more favorable attitudes enter into more or different kinds of contact with minority groups, or did different kinds of contact lead to differences in attitude? Moreover, there was the added problem that the information about contact was based on retrospective reports by the respondents, and memory is fallible. Further, there was no way of knowing what other influences may have affected attitudes. Nevertheless, these studies led to an extremely interesting hypothesis and a number of subhypotheses: that sheer frequency of contact with members of a minority ethnic group does not necessarily lead to favorable attitudes toward that group. Rather, contact is most likely to result in favorable attitudes if it is relatively intimate and if it takes place between individuals of equal status, if contact occurs with individuals who are similar to oneself in education or occupational level, and if it occurs in a setting in which all participants have equal status within the immediate situation.

Recognizing the limitations of such questionnaire studies, but eager to test the hypotheses they generated, investigators turned to existing social settings. A number of investigators arranged situations in which whites who did not ordinarily encounter able, well-educated Blacks had the opportunity to do so. For example, F. T. Smith (1943) arranged a program of two weekend visits to Harlem, in which teachers attending a summer session visited a hospital staffed primarily by Blacks, heard lectures by outstanding Blacks, and were entertained in the home of an upper-class Black family. He found marked favorable changes in attitudes following the experience. However, from the point of view of drawing inferences that could be generalized, this study (and others like it) had a serious drawback: the purpose of the program was to provide an opportunity to meet Black people, and the whites who took part did so voluntarily. It seems reasonable to suppose that voluntary participants in interracial activities are relatively unprejudiced to begin with, or at least, relatively open to change in attitude. Smith did examine a comparison group of teachers attending the same summer school who expressed an interest in taking part in the Harlem weekends but who, for various practical reasons, were unable to do so. He found that those who actually took part showed much more favorable attitude change than those who had expressed interest but did not actually go. Even disregarding the possibility that those deterred by practical obstacles were less motivated to participate, we can conclude only that people who voluntarily enter into situations of contact with a social group from which they are ordinarily segregated become more favorable in their attitudes as a result of the experience. This is important information, but it does not permit conclusions about the effects of contact when different groups are thrown together without choice—a more important issue in light of the state of American society today.

A number of investigators turned to ongoing social situations in which members of different racial groups were brought together in the context of their everyday activities, with little or no choice on their part. Brophy (1946) compared the attitudes of white merchant seamen who had never shipped with Blacks and those of seamen who had shipped with Blacks one or more times. Star, et al. (1949) compared the attitudes of white soldiers in companies having Black platoons with those of white soldiers in all white companies in the same regiment. Kramer (1951) and Winder (1952) compared the attitudes of white residents of neighborhoods that were at varying distances from areas into which substantial numbers of Blacks were moving; Irish (1952) compared the attitudes of whites who had Japanese-American neighbors with those who did not; Deutsch and Collins (1951) and Wilner, Walkley, and Cook (1955) compared the behavior and attitudes of white housewives living different distances from Blacks in public housing projects with different occupancy patterns. Harding and Hogrefe (1952) compared the attitudes of white department store employees in departments where there were no Black employees, in departments having Blacks in lower-status jobs, and in departments where whites and Blacks held the same jobs.

In none of these studies did the investigator have control over the conditions of contact or over the assignment of individuals to different situations. Likewise, there was no opportunity to assess attitudes before the contact occurred. Thus, there was no assurance that the differences in attitude found between groups differing in the extent of their contact with á minority group were attributable to the contact rather than to other factors. Individuals in different situations might have differed in their racial attitudes, or in other relevant characteristics, before the contact occurred. Nevertheless, this possibility was not nearly so great as in the earlier studies, since there was some clear and important motive—other than an interest in interracial association—for individuals to enter or remain in the situation that meant racial contact. The possibility remains, however, that extremely prejudiced whites would not have entered into situations that they knew might involve contact with nonwhites or might have left situations into which nonwhites had recently entered. Only in the army study, where individuals had no choice whatsoever, could this possibility be entirely ruled out.

field studies   A second advantage of the later field studies is that the investigators had a good deal of objective knowledge about the social situation. They knew, for example, whether or not a soldier was in a company that had Black platoons, whether a white housewife lived in an integrated or segregated housing project and how far her apartment was from the nearest Black family, or in which department an employee worked. And to the extent that these studies also made use of the individuals' own reports of their association with members of the minority group within the contact situation, they had the advantage of asking about a present situation rather than about the past, thus reducing the possibility of errors resulting from poor memory.

Perhaps the greatest problem in interpreting the findings of the field studies is that, in real life, conditions that may influence attitudes tend to be tied together, so that it is difficult to isolate the effects of any single condition or to test inferences about underlying processes (Brunswik, 1955, 1956). For example, in the army study, being in a company with a Black platoon provided an opportunity to observe Blacks at close quarters and thus to get more accurate information about them. It also involved sharing danger and working toward a common goal. It also carried the weight of official sanctioning.

Despite the limitations of any single study, in combination the mass of studies added up to rather substantial evidence about the effects of contact under varying conditions. On the whole, they supported the hypotheses suggested by the earlier studies about the importance of equal status and of the degree of intimacy of the contact. In addition, they suggested some new hypotheses: (1) that when contact takes place under conditions of competition or where the entry of members of a minority group is felt as a threat (for example, in the study of neighborhoods into which Blacks were moving), contact does not lead to favorable attitude change, and that anticipation of contact under such circumstances is likely to lead to negative attitude change; (2) that contact is especially likely to lead to favorable attitude change when it occurs under conditions of mutual interdependence in the face of a common danger; (3) that contact is more likely to lead to favorable attitude change if it is accompanied by a statement of policy by a respected authority; (4) that the attitude change tends to be limited to the particular group and the particular kind of situation in which the individual experienced contact with that group, with relatively little generalization to other groups or other situations.

Several investigators moved on to situations in which they had greater control and thus could eliminate more competing hypotheses that would explain their findings (see, for example, Cook, 1970). One of these groups (Sherif and his associates) concentrated on "field experiments"—situations that appeared to the participants to be natural "real-life" experiences, but in which the investigators were able to select the participants, control the conditions under which contact occurred, and decide which subjects should be exposed to which conditions.

Sherif (1958) carried out his studies in summer camps for boys. There were three studies, in three successive summers, in different geographical areas. The boys who attended the camps had no knowledge that they were taking part in an experiment. Throughout the experiment, the investigators were not identified as such but appeared simply as part of the staff. All of the manipulations of conditions were made within the framework of regular camp activities, and all of the observations were made unobtrusively.

The boys were all eleven or twelve years old, healthy, somewhat above average in intelligence, socially well adjusted, and from stable, white, Protestant, middle-class families. None of the boys knew each other before camp. In the first study, the boys were housed in one large bunkhouse for the first few days. Friendships developed very quickly. After a few days, the group was divided into two subgroups, each group living in a separate cabin. Before assignments to the subgroups were made, each boy was asked informally who his best friends in the camp were; as far as possible, best friends were separated. Thus, the investigators set up two similar groups without strong internal ties. Within a short time, each subgroup had developed a strong sense of unity and identity.

The investigators next attempted to develop conflict and hostility between the two groups in order to study the processes by which intergroup hostility develops, and in order to be sure they had antagonistic groups when they later set about trying to reduce the hostility. In developing intergroup hostility, the experimenters worked from the hypothesis that when two groups have conflicting aims the members of each group will become hostile toward the members of the other, even though both groups are made up of normal, well-adjusted individuals. To produce friction, the experimenters set up games, with the winning group to receive a prize. While the tournament started in a spirit of good sportsmanship, soon the boys began labelling members of the rival group as "sneaks" and "cheats"; they refused to have anything to do with members of the rival group, even turning against those they had earlier chosen as best friends. Simultaneously, there was a marked increase in solidarity within each group. When the boys again rated each other and indicated their best friends, the ratings of members of their own group were predominantly favorable, while those of the other group were predominantly negative. Almost all choices of friends were made *within* each subgroup.

In the first study, having created two hostile groups, the experimenters proceeded on the simple hypothesis that personal contact in enjoyable situations creates more favorable attitudes. They brought the two groups of boys together for a party, to see a movie, and similar events. But instead of fraternizing, the boys used these opportunities for further name-calling and fighting. There was no support for the investigators' hypothesis that personal contact with members of a disliked group in an enjoyable situation would lead to favorable attitudes. It should be noted, however, that the contact situations provided in the camp experiment were short and did not particularly encourage genuine association between members of the two groups. One may question whether the activities Sherif and his associates chose were adequate representations of the concept of personal contact.

The investigators next decided to test the hypothesis that, just as competition generates friction, working in a common endeavor should promote harmony. Therefore, in their next studies, having built up antagonism between the two groups, they created situations in which there were *superordinate goals* of great importance for both groups but which neither group could achieve without the help of the other. For example, they arranged a breakdown in the camp water supply, which necessitated checking the pipe that carried water to the camp from a distant source—a job that required the services of all the boys. On another occasion, the boys requested a movie, and were told that the camp could not afford to rent it; the two groups got together, figured out how much each would have to contribute, chose the film by vote, and watched it together, peacefully.

These joint efforts did not dispel the hostility all at once. Gradually, however, the series of cooperative acts reduced friction and conflict, and friendly behavior appeared in both ratings and choice of friends. The investigators concluded that hostility between groups can be reduced by placing them in situations where they must work together in order to achieve important common goals.

What were the advantages of these procedures, as compared with studies of relations between different ethnic groups in naturally occurring settings? At first glance, relations between artificially formed groups of middle-class white boys may not seem to have much relevance for the understanding of race relations in the larger society. But this very feature of the experiment overcame a number of problems encountered in natural situations where the investigator has no control. Recognizing the problem of prior attitudes, investigators in natural settings usually try to get supplementary information about attitudes prior to intergroup contact. Yet, these inferences remain uncertain at best. In the camp experiments, Sherif and his associates selected boys who at first presumably had *no* attitudes toward each other, since they did not know each other and were similar in major background characteristics; by assignment, they established groups that they knew were not hostile toward each other and within which there were no strong internal ties; then, by setting up conditions of competition, they created groups whose members disliked the members of the rival group. In other words, uncertainty about initial attitudes was eliminated.

A second advantage of Sherif's procedure was selection of boys who did not have personal or social difficulties and who were similar to each other in race, religion, intelligence, and socioeconomic status. This fact eliminated the possibility that other differences among the individuals whose attitudes are being compared may have led to the observed differences in intergroup attitudes.

A third advantage of Sherif's procedure was that, for the period of the experiment, the boys lived entirely within the camp setting. Changes that took place could reasonably be attributed to experiences in the camp, without concern for other possible influences. Such situations are rare in everyday life. The city council member in the midst of a reelection campaign, the school bus driver, the resident of a neighborhood into which nonwhites are moving, are at the same time subject to many other influences which may affect their attitudes.

Fourth, the investigators were able to insure that conditions corresponding to their abstract concepts actually prevailed, by setting up situations of competition and cooperation. Conditions in naturally occurring situations may or may not correspond reasonably well to the concept an investigator has in mind. Controlling the conditions has an advantage.

Finally, it was possible in the camp studies to observe a great deal of what went on, thus giving insight into the processes of attitude development and change. In principle, it is possible, but difficult, to carry out studies of attitude change in naturally occurring situations by observation over a period of time (see Cook, 1970). The usual procedure has been to interview individuals at one point in time and rely either on their descriptions or inferences about what actually takes place on a day-by-day basis. Sherif and his associates, however, were dealing with a small number of boys in a concentrated setting, in which the investigators had control over the occurrence of events that were likely to produce significant interaction. In addition, they were able to observe unobtrusively and to introduce ingenious observational methods that could not easily be used in uncontrolled situations.

Note, however, that a paradox appears as a result of the increasing sophistication in the design of the studies. As we become more certain of the conceptual adequacy of the measurements we are taking, we do not become increasingly certain of the extent to which we can generalize our findings to broader social groups. Indeed, the more carefully we eliminate alternative explanations for results, the less certain we can be about the applicability of findings to other groups and other situations.

II. CONSIDERATIONS IN DESIGNING STUDIES ABOUT "CAUSAL" RELATIONSHIPS AMONG VARIABLES

We have discussed the above studies in considerable detail in order to illustrate the problems involved in testing a proposition that one or more conditions influences one or more outcomes. It is important to note that we rarely think in terms of a single "cause" producing a single "effect"; rather it can nearly always be assumed that a number of conditions influence an outcome. In technical terminology, as we noted in Chapter 2, a condition that is hypothesized to influence another is referred to as the independent variable (the "cause"); a condition that is thought of as being influenced is referred to as the dependent variable (the "effect"). In abstract discussions throughout this book, we shall frequently refer to a presumed independent variable as X and a presumed dependent variable as Y.

A. Concomitant variation

concomitant variation

A basic condition necessary to support a hypothesis that one variable influences another is that the two must vary together in the way specified in the hypothesis. Individuals who differ with respect to X, for instance, must also differ with respect to Y. This is sometimes referred to as "concomitant variation." All that is involved in the notion of concomitant variation is the simple common-sense idea that unless two variables are found to go together there is no basis for inferring that one may be a cause of the other.

---

[1] In this section and throughout the rest of this chapter, we have drawn heavily on the work of Campbell (1957) and Campbell and Stanley (1966). These authors discuss the issues and various solutions in considerably more detail than is done in this book; the reader who is interested in pursuing these questions in greater depth is referred to these papers and others by the same authors.

Sherif, in the first camp experiment, for example, tested two hypotheses: (1) when two groups have competitive goals, the members will become mutually hostile; (2) personal contact between members of two hostile groups in enjoyable situations leads to a reduction of hostility and the development of friendly feelings. With competition (condition X), the members of two groups did in fact become extremely hostile (characteristic Y) toward members of the rival group; thus the first hypothesis remained tenable. However, once having built up hostility between the two groups, simply bringing them together in enjoyable situations did not reduce hostility. Thus, the second relationship was not found, at least under the conditions in which it was tested.

The later camp experiments tested a third hypothesis, that joint activity toward the achievement of "superordinate goals" desired by both groups but not achievable by either one alone (variable X) leads to a reduction of hostility and development of friendly feelings (variable Y). It was found that after the boys participated in such activities they did in fact become less hostile toward members of the other group and more friendly toward them; thus this hypothesis remained tenable.

These may be thought of as hypotheses about the effects of three values of one independent variable (the degree to which a situation encouraged competition versus cooperation) on one dependent variable (degree of hostility or friendliness between two groups). The three values of X are: situations in which the two groups had competing goals which could only be won by one group at the expense of the other (X_1); pleasant activities not requiring either competition or cooperation (X_2); situations requiring cooperation in order to achieve goals desired by both groups (X_3). The predicted outcomes concerned the degree of hostility versus friendliness. Looked at in this way, the more general hypothesis, that the conditions under which contact occurs influence intergroup attitudes and behavior, was supported for the two extreme values of X (situations with competitive goals and situations where goals could be achieved only by cooperation) but not for an intermediate value of X (conditions where group goals did not require either competition or cooperation). The fact that the position on Y associated with X was *reversed* when the value of X was reversed not only strengthened the evidence of concomitant variation but increased the plausibility of the interpretation that X had a causal influence on Y.

B. Plausible alternative explanations to the hypothesis

If X and Y are found not to be associated, it is very unlikely that one influences, or is a cause of, the other, at least under the circumstances of the particular study. If they do vary together, however, this covariation is by no means conclusive proof that X influences Y; other plausible explanations for differences with respect to Y must be considered. In principle, of course, the number of possible influences on Y is infinite. In practice, however, the variables (other than X) that are most likely to have affected Y in any given study can be grouped into a limited number of categories. Among the most important are: (1) past experiences or relatively enduring characteristics of the individuals being studied, including the possibility that they differed with respect to Y before the occurrence of X; (2) contemporaneous events other than exposure to X; (3) maturational or developmental changes; and (4) aspects of the research procedure other than the intended independent variable X. Many of these possible alternative explanations have been mentioned in the discussion of problems of interpreting studies concerning the relationship between contact with members of a minority group and attitudes toward that group. In this section we shall discuss the major types of alternative hypotheses more systematically.

1. Past experiences or relatively enduring characteristics of the subjects

Initial position on Y. One of the most likely possibilities is that the groups of subjects may have differed in their position on Y even before exposure to X. It may even be that these initial differences with respect to Y led some subjects to expose themselves to condition X and others to avoid it. The early studies of the effects of personal contact on attitudes of majority-group members toward members of minority groups illustrate this possibility. This problem occurs whenever there is self-selection—that is, when individuals volunteer to participate in a treatment the nature of which they know in advance. The studies focusing on naturally occurring differences in contact offered greater protection against this possibility since in each of them the individuals entered into the contact situation for some compelling reason (desire for adequate housing, for a job, or another reason) other than any interest in interracial association. In addition, in some of these studies the investigators obtained retrospective reports of prior attitudes. Nevertheless, in most of these studies it was not possible to rule out completely the possibility that extremely prejudiced people had avoided the contact situations.

Past experiences or characteristics other than initial position on the dependent variable may also influence individuals' positions on that variable after exposure to the presumed independent variable. This possibility, too, must be taken into account before differences on the dependent variable can be attributed to differences on the independent variable. For example, in studies based on correlations between individuals' attitudes toward minority groups and their reports of their contact with members of those groups, it may be that those who have had a good deal of equal-status contact with minority-group members differ from those who have not had such contact in their general attitudes toward people. Or, they may differ in their openness to new experiences, in education, socioeconomic status, the geographical area in which they grew up—any of which might have led to differences in their attitudes toward minority groups, independently of the extent of their contact with minority-group members, or which might have influenced the extent to which they entered into such contact. These possibilities are present also in studies based on comparison of groups known to be exposed to different degrees of contact with members of minority groups in "real-life" situations.

2. Other contemporaneous events

Life does not stand still while a study is taking place, nor are people usually exposed to variation in only one condition at a time. Usually many other things are happening to the subjects in addition to the specific influence the investigator is studying, and some of these other things may influence that dependent variable. For example, in the study of white merchant seamen (Brophy, 1946), each man belonged to either of two different unions, one of which had a militant antidiscrimination policy, while the other did not. As would be expected, the members of the union with the antidiscrimination policy were more likely to have shipped with Blacks. Moreover, the longer they had been in the union, the more often they had been members of interracial crews. Thus, it was possible that exposure to the union's policy and educational program, rather than (or together with) the experience of working and living closely with Blacks on board ship, was responsible for their more favorable attitudes.

Problems of this sort are not limited to studies concerned with past events or to any particular type of research design. Singer (1968), in an experimental study of the effects of humor in reducing aggression, conducted experimental sessions from April through September of 1963. His subjects were Black, the materials used to arouse aggression had to do with the treatment of Black people in the United States, the humorist was Black, and in one of the experimental conditions his jokes involved hostile humor directed at whites. But the summer of 1963 was filled with headline-making events affecting race relations. In April there were riots in Birmingham, Alabama; in August there was a massive civil rights march on Washington, D.C.; in early September a Black church in Birmingham was bombed, killing four children. These events so greatly influenced the mood of the subjects that the investigator divided the analysis of his data into two time periods, early and late summer, and found markedly different effects of hostile humor in the two time periods.

3. Maturational or developmental changes

Not only do outer events impinge on individuals, but there may be inner developmental processes at work, independently of X (the assumed causal variable), that influence Y (the dependent variable). Young children given special training in motor skills may show considerable improvement, but the improvement might have been equally great without the special training, if the skill depended on physiological maturation that coincided with the training period. Counseling of college students may lead to an increase in their self-confidence, but self-confidence may also increase as a result of additional social experience or of the experience of being on one's own. Institutionalization of elderly persons may be followed by rather rapid physical and mental deterioration, but such deterioration might have occurred as a function of physiological changes associated with old age, quite aside from institutionalization.

Again, this problem is not limited to particular study designs, though it is more obvious in studies that extend over long periods of time. But even in an hour's experimental session, subjects may become tired, hungry, or bored, leading to changes in Y, independently of X.

4. Aspects of the research procedure

Reactivity is an unwanted influence on a subject's responses, created by calling attention to the fact that this subject is being studied. For example, subjects may react by giving the response they think the investigator wants, or by trying to outwit the investigator. It does not matter whether the guesses about the investigator's purpose are right or wrong, or whether they are done to help or hinder. The reactive responses may be mixed up with the effect of X on Y. The most common of such influences are the measurement process, the way in which X is introduced or presented to the subjects, and the general setting of the study.

The measurement process. Measurement procedures may directly influence subjects' positions on the characteristic being measured or may affect reaction to the independent variable. This is especially likely if the measurements are administered before exposure to the independent variable, or if they are repeated. For example, it has been found repeatedly that scores on the second administration of an intelligence or aptitude test tend to be higher than on the first administration, presumably because of some *practice effect* or learning that occurs as a result of having taken the test previously. Thus, tests administered before and after a remedial program are likely to show improvement because of the practice effect rather than because of the educational program. An attitude or opinion questionnaire administered just before subjects are shown a film intended to influence those attitudes or opinions may sensitize subjects to aspects of the film that they might not otherwise have noticed. In the study of the effects of humor on the reduction of aggression mentioned earlier (Singer, 1968), the first step was to arouse different degrees of aggression in the subjects. To do this, two different tape recordings were presented about the position of Blacks in the United States, one highly emotional and inflammatory, the other calm and objective. To check whether these communications had the intended effect, half the subjects filled out a "mood checklist" immediately after hearing the communication and before hearing the humorous record-ing, while the other half received no checklist. Responses to the checklist indicated that the communications had indeed been successful in arousing different degrees of aggression. However, responses to the checklist itself reduced tension and aggressive impulses and substantially influenced the reaction to the humor.

Questionnaires and checklists are not the only measurement procedures that may be "reactive." The presence of an observer making notes, or the knowledge that a conversation is being tape recorded, or the suspicion that there is an observer behind a one-way screen may affect behavior. As Webb, *et al.* (1966) suggest, in a study concerned with weight reduction, initial weighing in may have a motivational effect that influences subjects' food consumption independently of the planned treatments. Evans, *et al.* (1973) study of dental health habits found that the assessment of oral cleanliness through use of disclosing wafers had effects on dental habits that outweighed those of independent variables (communications regard-ing dental hygiene).

Other aspects of the research procedure.   Not only are the measurement procedures potentially influential, but the outcome may also be affected by other aspects of the research procedure that are at least conceptually unre-lated to the independent variable in which the investigator is interested. **Hawthorne** The often cited "Hawthorne effect" is an example. In this research, the **effect** investigators (Roethlisberger and Dickson, 1939) were attempting to study the effects on productivity of variations in work conditions, such as hours of work, rest periods, lighting, and methods of pay. These variations were applied, over a period of more than a year, to a small work group in a large factory. To the surprise of the investigators, the production rate rose stead-ily during the entire period, whether the work hours were lengthened or shortened, rest periods fewer or more frequent, and so on. Their final con-clusion was that the most influential factor was the high morale engendered by the awareness of being a special experimental group—a totally unin-tended effect as far as the original research purpose was concerned.

A person asked to fill out an attitude questionnaire, presented with a communication on the topic covered by the questionnaire, and then asked to repeat the questionnaire or a similar one, must be dull indeed if he or she does not perceive that the communication was intended to have some effect on attitude. The possibility of question reactivity constitutes a highly plausible alternative to the investigator's hypothesis that the communica-tion influenced the attitude.

Even considerably less transparent research arrangements may still influ-ence behavior and thus constitute plausible alternative hypotheses about the determinants of the behavior. In fact, as a number of writers have pointed out, when the research procedures are out of the ordinary and do not clearly suggest the investigator's purpose, subjects are likely to make up their own hypotheses about the research purpose. To the extent that different subjects arrive at different hypotheses, and to the extent that these differ from the investigator's focus of interest, the resultant influences on behavior may not systematically affect the outcome, but they may well obscure whatever influences the independent variable might otherwise have had. (Aronson and Carlsmith, 1968, pp. 61–70, have an excellent discussion of "demand characteristics" of the experimental situation as possible sources of bias and thus of plausible alternative hypotheses about the factors influencing position on the dependent variable. For more detailed discussions of specific ways in which aspects of research procedure may affect outcomes, see McDavid, 1965; Orne, 1962; Riecken, 1962; Rosenberg, 1965; Silverman, 1965.)

demand characteristics

III. HOW DIFFERENT RESEARCH DESIGNS REDUCE THE PLAUSIBILITY OF ALTERNATIVE HYPOTHESES

A major function of research design in the testing of causal hypotheses is to reduce the plausibility of rival hypotheses—that is, to reduce the likelihood that, in the particular study, one or more classes of interfering factors might account for the obtained results. Research designs differ in the ways they do this. In the following sections we shall discuss three major classes of research designs—true experimental designs, quasi-experiments, and nonexperimental studies—from the point of view of the protection they offer against these alternative hypotheses.

experiment   What exactly *is* an experiment? Experiments are studies in which the investigator has control over the independent variable and over the assignment of subjects to different conditions. The ideal true experiment is a controlled laboratory study in which the effects of the independent variables are assessed while the other possible, confounding effects are ruled out. However, experiments can be carried out in the "real world," if the experimenter possesses enough control over the environment.

A. How various basic features of experimental designs help rule out alternative hypotheses

Serious problems in interpreting relationships among variables arise from the possibilities that the presumed independent variable *may in fact have been brought about by the presumed variable* (rather than the reverse) or that both of these variables may have been the result of some other factor. For example, in studies based on self-reports of contact with members of minority groups and of attitudes toward those groups, it is found that individuals who report more contact have more favorable attitudes, but one cannot be sure that the contact led to the favorable attitude. People who already have favorable attitudes toward a group may be more likely to enter into personal association with members of that group. Or, as in the study of merchant seamen (Brophy, 1946), membership in a union with a strong nondiscrimination policy may have led both to increased contact (a greater number of voyages on ships with racially mixed crews) and to reduction in prejudice. When the investigator controls and manipulates the independent variable, these sources of ambiguity are eliminated, or at least greatly reduced. As Aronson and Carlsmith (1968, p. 8) remarked: "The experimenter knows what caused X—he did."

A related advantage is that the experimenter's control makes it possible to focus on the specific factor of interest. Experiences in everyday life are always complex, and variables tend to come in bunches. For example, situations in which members of different ethnic or racial groups work cooperatively toward common goals are likely to be marked by social norms favorable to intergroup association, by equality of status within the situation, and by opportunities for getting to know members of the other group. If one is trying to discover the relative importance of these various factors, it is difficult without sufficient control of the situation to be able to manipulate these variables separately.

Laboratory studies of people are artificial. Efforts to manipulate social and psychological variables are typically pale and contrived, compared to real situations. Yet those real situations are so complex that it is difficult or impossible to separate out factors, and, in real life, people select what they do, when they do it, and with whom.

Laboratory experiments, however, help eliminate numerous plausible alternative explanations that would be present in studies conducted in less fully controlled, naturally occurring situations. The degree of control is achieved because one can insure that subjects assigned to different treatments are alike in all respects except by chance variation. While subjects in experiments are thus plucked out of their social environment, the "artificial" laboratory setting removes the potentially confounding effects of a host of subject characteristics.

Another advantage of experimental manipulation of conditions is a very practical one. Events of interest to the investigator may not occur very often in real life. Moreover, the investigator usually has no way of knowing when and where they are going to occur. In an experiment, where the investigator can produce the kinds of conditions wanted, crucial events can be arranged at a time and place where observation and measurement are possible.

B. Control groups

control group   A control group provides essential protection against the possibility that factors other than the experimental treatment may have affected the dependent variable. Control groups may also be used to provide evidence relevant to specific alternative hypotheses that seem especially plausible in a particular study.

Sometimes pretest-posttest studies of a single group exposed to an experimental treatment, without a control group, are carried out. Such studies offer no protection against any of the possible alternative explanations for a change from the pre- to postmeasure, and therefore, are uninterpretable as evidence about the relationship between X and Y. A review by Campbell and Dunnette (1968) of research on the effects of sensitivity-training groups ("T groups") provides a striking example. They noted that a number of such studies focused on changes in members' self-perceptions during training, particularly with respect to their actual self-image (the way they describe themselves as behaving or feeling), their ideal self-image (the way they would like to be), and their impressions of other members of their group. They summarized one study in which such measures were administered to members of six different T groups, without controls. For the six groups, the changes were in the direction of greater agreement between subjects' descriptions of themselves and other members' descriptions of them— presumably outcomes in keeping with the goals of the T-group experience. These reviewers then described a rather representative study with three different T groups, *plus* a control group for each, drawn from the same college population. The findings for the three T groups were essentially the same as those in the first study. However, and this is the crucial point, the control groups showed similar changes, and there were no differences between the experimental and control groups on the postmeasures (Campbell and Dunnette, p. 90). Changes in comparable groups not exposed to the experimental experience suggested that the changes might be attributed simply to repeated taking of the same tests. Whatever the experimental variable, a change in a group exposed to it might have resulted from the effects of the pretest, from maturational processes, from other contemporaneous events, from the method of selection of the subjects, or from aspects of the research procedure other than the variable in which the investigator is interested. Although the use of a control group cannot completely rule out all of these other possible alternatives, it does reduce their plausibility.

C. Assignment of subjects to conditions

In order to provide protection against alternative hypotheses, the control group must, of course, be initially equivalent to the experimental group. Clearly, the task of creating or of unearthing groups that are equivalent in all respects is an impossible one; the goal can only be approximated. In true experimental designs, the basic safeguard against differences between experimental and control groups that might lessen the validity of inferences randomization about the effects of the experimental treatment is *randomization*.

Random assignment of subjects to different treatment conditions (or of experimenters to different conditions or subjects) entails the same *principles* as those involved in selecting a simple random sample for a descriptive study (see Chapter 4). The assignment procedures must give each subject the same chance as that of any other subject of being assigned to any given condition. Assignment based, either consciously or unconsciously, on the investigator's judgment, or the subject's preference, or any other systematic bias is ruled out. For example, one may flip a coin for each subject, assigning that person to the experimental group if it comes up "heads," to the control group if it comes up "tails." Or one may number each person and then, by using a table of random numbers, select as many cases as are wanted for the experimental group and assign the remaining ones to the control group.

The chance assignment of individuals to the different conditions precludes the possibility of initial systematic differences between the groups selected. This does not mean that the experimental and control groups will be exactly alike, but rather that whatever differences exist before the introduction of the experimental variable are the result of chance alone. The rules of probability make it possible to specify the extent of differences that might be expected by chance in the long run (that is, if the selection were repeated a large number of times). If, after one group has been exposed to the experimental treatment, the two groups are found to differ more than would be expected by chance, one may infer that the experimental variable led to the difference. This inference, of course, is tentative, subject to the possibility that some other factor may have led to the difference.

R. A. Fisher (1951), one of the outstanding figures in the development of experimental design, has pointed out that:

> . . . the uncontrolled causes which may influence the result (of an experiment) are always strictly innumerable. When any such cause is named, it is usually perceived that, by increased labour and expense, it could be largely eliminated. Too frequently it is assumed that such refinements constitute improvements to the experiment. . . . whatever degree of care and experimental skill is expended in equalising the conditions, other than the one under test, which are liable to affect the result, this equalisation must always be to a greater or less extent incomplete, and in many important practical cases will certainly be grossly defective . . . the simple precaution of randomisation will suffice to guarantee the validity of the test of significance, by which the result of the experiment is to be judged.[2]

Campbell and Stanley (1963, p. 15), conceding that randomization is "a less than perfect way" of assuring the initial equivalence of the groups to be compared, have also said: "It is nonetheless the only way of doing so, and the essential way." They explained that they made this statement so unequivocally in order to make clear their disagreement with the view that matching, without randomization, is an acceptable way of securing equivalent groups. Matching refers here to pairing subjects who are equal on some relevant variables, and then placing one in each group. In fact, they maintained that matching groups is more often a source of mistaken inference than it is a help to valid inference.[3]

---

[2] For a discussion of tests of significance, see Chapter 14.

[3] Their reasons for this position involved statistical considerations beyond the scope of this book. The reader who is interested in pursuing this point is referred to Campbell and Stanley (1963, pp. 49–50).

Neither randomization nor any other known procedure can completely rule out the possibility that some factor other than X—either an initial difference between the groups or something occurring during the course of the experiment—may have led to the difference in Y. Thus the inference that X led to, or influenced, or caused, Y must always be made tentatively and be held subject to possible revision or change in the light of later evidence. In this sense, experiments do not demonstrate causality any more or less than other techniques.

Randomization can be done with *any* pool of subjects. It is an important **internal validity** component of the *internal* validity of an experiment (which asks was there **external validity** an effect of the independent variable). Generalizability, or *external* validity, involves questions of the representativeness of the subject pool and of the experimental events. The efficacy of randomization for internal validity depends, of course, on keeping the randomized group intact. A threat to validity occurs if there are dropouts from the groups—a point of great concern in randomized field trials, for example, of changes in living habits in relation to development of heart disease.

In summary, random assignment to treatment and control groups is an important aspect of true experiments. In itself, random selection does not actually control any variable, but rather mixes up all the characteristics that differentiate people and pours them into the experimental and control groups, thus pulling apart any ties that might exist between unwanted variables and the dependent variable.

IV. SOME COMMON EXPERIMENTAL DESIGNS

Of the numerous possible experimental designs, we shall describe only a few of the simplest and most common.[4] There is as yet no completely standard terminology for identifying experimental designs; we shall refer to "after-only" designs and "before-after" designs. In these designations, **"after-only"** "before" and "after" refer to the times at which measurements of the de- **designs** pendent variable are made in relation to the introduction of the experi- **"before-after"** mental variable. In other words, "before" indicates a "pretest;" "after," a **designs** "posttest." In presenting designs, we shall use the following notation:

X indicates exposure of a group or an individual to an experimental variable or event.
Y indicates some process of assessment of the experimental group with respect to the dependent variable or some characteristic or characteristics that seem likely to be related to it:
Y_1 indicates assessment *before* the introduction or occurrence of X.
Y_2 indicates assessment *after* the introduction or occurrence of X.

---

[4] For discussions of more complex designs, see: Cox (1958a), Lindquist (1953), Solomon (1949), and Solomon and Lessac (1968).

Y' indicates assessment of a control group with respect to the dependent variable.

Y'' and Y''' indicate assessment of additional control groups with respect to the dependent variable.

Subscripts $_1$ and $_2$ appended to Y', and so on, indicate assessments of the control group or groups at times corresponding to the assessment of the experimental group.

R indicates random assignment of individuals to experimental and control groups.

A. After-only design[5]

This design may be diagrammed as follows:

Experimental group: R X Y_2
Control Group: R Y'_2

Individuals are randomly assigned to the experimental or control group at some time *before* introduction of the experimental variable. Neither group is measured with respect to the dependent variable before exposure to the experimental variable. The experimental group is exposed to the experimental variable; the control group is not. Both groups are measured with respect to the dependent variable at some time after the experimental group is exposed to the experimental variable.

In this design, the hypothesis that X influences Y is or is not tenable is determined by comparing Y in the experimental group after exposure to variable X, with Y' in the control group, which has not been exposed to X. Thus, we would compare Y_2 with Y'_2.

How does this design give us evidence from which we can plausibly infer that X has influenced Y? Let us examine this question in the light of our earlier listing of the major kinds of evidence relevant to this question.

Concomitant variation. If Y_2 and Y'_2 differ significantly, we conclude that, at least under the conditions of this experiment, X and Y vary together, since the group exposed to X differs subsequently from the group not exposed to X; thus the hypothesis remains tenable. If Y_2 and Y'_2 do not differ significantly, it is clear that in this study exposure or nonexposure to X is not associated with differences in Y; thus we conclude that the hypothesis that X influences Y is implausible.

Evidence about the direction of influence. The possibility that Y may

---

[5] For the convenience of those readers who want to consider the various designs and their advantages and disadvantages in more detail by consulting Campbell and Stanley (1963), we shall indicate which of their designs each one we discuss corresponds to. This "after-only" design is identical with their Design 6, the "posttest only control group design."

have influenced X, rather than vice versa, is greatly reduced, on the following grounds.

1. As discussed earlier, random assignment of subjects to the experimental and control groups makes it unlikely that the two groups differed with respect to Y before exposure to X. Moreover, under conditions of random assignment, probability theory tells us to what extent they might differ by chance in terms of their initial position on Y, and the test of significance of the difference between Y_2 and Y'_2 takes this into account.
2. The fact that the experimenter introduced X (or knew in advance how and when it was to be introduced and that subjects were randomly assigned to conditions) is presumptive evidence that it was the experimenter (or other controlling agent), rather than Y, that produced X.

What about evidence that other factors were responsible for differences in Y? Random assignment is the best assurance that the groups did not differ initially in characteristics that might be associated with differences in Y. The assumption is that other contemporaneous events are the same for both groups; thus they cannot account for the difference between Y_2 and Y'_2. However, there is a possibility that other events may *interact* with X to affect Y; this design does not take account of this possibility. Given random assignment, the groups are likely to be equivalent in initial position on any maturational or developmental dimensions likely to affect Y. If any changes on these dimensions have taken place during the course of the study, they affect both groups equally. Again, the possibility of interaction between such changes and X, in their effect on Y, is not taken into account.

Finally, this design includes the possibility that something in the research procedures other than the intended experimental variable has influenced Y. However, by dispensing with a premeasure of Y, it very much reduces the likelihood that the *measurement* procedures may influence Y.

An example of an after-only study. There has been a long series of investigations into the question of what factors induce aggressive behavior in people. Of demonstrable social importance, aggression against others has been studied in relation to personality, social norms, authority relationships, exposure to mass media, and situational inducements. An extensive accumulation of laboratory research on aggression has provided important information about conditions that induce subjects to harm others.

Berkowitz and his associates have investigated a variety of cues that serve to trigger or inhibit aggressive response (see, for example, Berkowitz, 1965). A standard measure of aggression, utilized in many experiments, is the number or intensity of electric shocks delivered by the subject to another person. Emotional arousal and/or situational cues are manipulated by the experimenter as independent variables, then subjects are provided with a plausible opportunity to deliver shocks to someone else. In a typical after-only design, the shock measures are taken only once—following exposure to the independent variables. Since the investigator does not assess the subject's propensity to give shocks prior to the treatment, comparing posttest scores across groups assumes pretest equivalence, within the limits of chance variation. Hence, random assignment to the treatments is crucial.

A study by Berkowitz and Alioto (1973) is illustrative. Their hypothesis was that the interpretation of observed events affects the strength of aggressive reactions produced by the events. More generally, aggressive behavior is thought to be a function of *both* the disposition to aggress and situational cues that promote aggression. Aggressive propensities can be inhibited by proper situational cues. In the study, the experimenters first sought to arouse aggressive impulses, then provide (via films) cues that facilitated or inhibited aggression, and then finally give subjects an opportunity to shock a partner. In contrast, control subjects were given neutral cues plus the opportunity to deliver shocks. For the experimental subjects, the procedure included, first, a bogus learning task with a partner (actually a confederate of the investigator) who evaluated a series of the subject's proposals by delivering electric shock. By using excessive shock, the investigators thus created angry subjects. Next the subject viewed an aggressive film of a prize fight or a football game. However, the film was described as either an aggressive, vengeful encounter or as a professional match without emotional involvement of the participants. Two different sets were thereby induced, one aggressively toned, the other neutral. Finally, the subject returned to the initial task with the "partner," except now in the position of evaluator who delivered performance ratings by means of shock. Number and duration of shocks provided the dependent measure. In the control condition, the subjects saw an exciting but aggressively neutral film, then served as evaluators in the shock situation.

As an experimental design, this study required two treatment conditions with subjects disposed to aggress, thereby permitting comparison of the aggressive and neutral interpretation of the same events (the films). The control group served as a base-line condition in which subjects were neither angry (at least not deliberately made angry) nor given interpretations of stimuli with aggressive content. As hypothesized, those angered subjects who had been given an aggressive set displayed the most aggression, with controls showing the least. In this design, potentially reactive premeasures are avoided. All effects are inferred by comparison of the groups' postmeasures, with the experimenters assuming no systematic differences at the onset.

B. Before-after design

In its most common form, this design may be diagrammed as follows:

$$\text{Experimental group:} \quad R \; Y_1 \; X \; Y_2$$
$$\text{Control Group:} \quad\quad R \; Y'_1 \quad\; Y'_2$$

The difference between this design and the preceding one is that both the experimental and control groups are measured with respect to Y (or to some variable or variables thought related to Y) *before* exposure of the experimental group to X. As in the preceding design, assignment of individuals to experimental and control groups is made on a random basis. Although the position of R in the above diagram suggests that random assignment is made before the first measurement this is not always the case. The time relationship between assignment to treatment conditions and the preexposure measurement depends on the requirements of the particular study and the reason for use of a premeasure.

In this design, if the same measuring instrument is used for the before and after measures, one evaluates the hypothesis that X influences Y by comparing the extent of *change* from pre- to postmeasure on the part of the experimental group with change in the control group from pre- to postmeasure. In other words, one compares $(Y_2—Y_1)$ with $(Y'_2—Y'_1)$. However, if different instruments are used for the before and after measures of Y, or if the before measure is of some characteristic other than Y but thought to be related to it, it is not possible to compute change scores. In this case, judgment of the tenability of the hypothesis is based on comparison of Y_2 with Y'_2, as in the after-only experiment. In either case, more complicated statistical treatments may be used to increase the sensitivity of the experiment by taking into account initial differences in position on Y or in the variable measured in the pretest.

Since random assignment provides reasonable assurance of the initial equivalence of groups, why does an investigator go to the trouble of obtaining an initial measure? There are a number of reasons. First, the investigator may want to increase the sensitivity of the experiment by taking into account how much room there is for change on the dependent variable. For example, in an experiment designed to change attitudes toward some object or group in a favorable direction, individuals who are already favorable cannot show as much favorable change as those who are initially unfavorable. In studies where the cost of exposing subjects to the experimental condition is high, it is uneconomical to include subjects whose initial position leaves little room for change in the predicted direction. Thus a study of racial attitude change may wish to use initial measures of racial attitudes to identify a pool of potential subjects who are *sufficiently prejudiced* so that there is room for the interracial contact involved in the experimental sessions to have an effect. From this pool, the subjects can be randomly assigned to the two conditions.

Even in situations where it does not seem feasible or desirable to limit the pool of potential subjects in this way, it may still be useful to have a before measure to determine limits of possible change on the dependent variable and to take it into account in evaluating the effects of the experimental variable.

Second, the hypothesis with which the study is concerned may specify initial position on the dependent variable as conditioning the effect of the major experimental variable. For example, the hypothesis may state that an antiwar film will have a greater effect on persons who are initially neutral or opposed to war than on those who consider war necessary for national defense or an appropriate means of settling international disputes.

Even if the major hypothesis of the study does not refer to initial position on the dependent variable, the investigators may wish to analyze the data to see whether the experimental treatment has different effects on persons who were initially at different positions on the dependent variable. If this is to be done, the investigators must of course have a measure of the subjects' positions before subjects are exposed to the experimental treatment. To be interpretable, such comparisons should be made between individuals in the experimental group who started with certain initial positions and those in the *control group* who started with comparable positions.[6]

Finally, despite the general effectiveness of random assignment in assuring initial equivalence of groups, it is, as Campbell and Stanley commented a "less than perfect" way of doing so. This is especially true when small numbers of cases are used. Statistical tests of significance take into account the probability that random assignment has not yielded initially equivalent groups, thus protecting the investigators against concluding that the experimental variable has had an effect when, in fact, the differences are due to initial chance differences between the groups. But they do not protect against the opposite problem—that the groups initially differed in such a way as to *obscure* actual effects of the experimental variable. A before measure can be used to increase the sensitivity of the experiment by increasing the initial similarity of the groups beyond the extent provided by random assignment.

Nonequivalent randomly assigned groups occurred in a program of remedial preschool experience for children from poor backgrounds carried out by Susan Gray and her associates (Gray and Klaus, 1965, 1970; Klaus and Gray, 1968). In a pilot study involving a ten-week summer program just before entrance into first grade, children of the appropriate age whose homes and parents met criteria for cultural deprivation were randomly assigned to an experimental group who participated in the program or a control group who did not. It turned out, however, that the control group was significantly higher than the experimental group in Stanford-Binet IQ *before* the experimental group received the special summer training. This initial superiority of the control group complicated interpretation of the finding that the two groups did not differ in scores on the Metropolitan Achievement Test at the end of the first grade (Klaus and Gray, 1968, p. 2).

In order to avoid such dilemmas, if it is possible to secure an initial measure of the dependent variable or some characteristic believed to be

---

[6] For explanation of reasons for this, see Campbell and Stanley (1966, pp. 10–11 and p. 15).

related to it, the experimenter may decide to supplement random assignment by matching. For example, in a study such as the above, if it is possible to secure the relevant measure before assigning children to the various groups, the experimenter may set up pairs of children matched as nearly as possible on IQ and then by random procedure determine which child within each pair is assigned to which treatment condition.[7] Note, however, that in this example, matching is used in conjunction with randomization, not as a substitute for it.

Even if the investigator does not use the premeasure in the process of assigning individuals to groups, the sensitivity of the experiment may be increased by taking account of initial differences in the process of analyzing the data (for example, by an analysis of covariance). In such an analysis the difference in final position on Y that is attributable to differences in *initial* position on Y or its surrogate is, in effect, separated out by statistical means, leaving the remaining difference as an indication of the effect of X.[8]

Clearly, *matching* groups on the basis of some initial measure as a supplement to random assignment requires measurement before individuals are assigned to experimental or control groups or to various treatment conditions. However, statistical procedures for taking account of initial differences can be used equally validly whether the premeasure was made before or after assignment to treatment conditions. The above discussion suggests that a before-after design may provide a better basis than an after-only one for inference about the effects of X on Y, primarily by strengthening the evidence that the experimental and control groups did not differ initially with respect to Y or, if in spite of random assignment they did differ, making it possible to take account of this difference in the course of analysis of the data. Thus, it reduces still further the possibility that differences with respect to Y after the experimental treatment are attributable to initial differences in Y rather than to exposure or nonexposure to X.

How does the before-after design compare with the after-only design in providing the other kinds of evidence from which inferences about causality can be drawn?

Concomitant variation. The before-after experiment, like the after-only experiment, provides evidence as to whether X and Y vary together; in the before-after study, this evidence comes from comparison of the extent of *change* on the part of the experimental and control groups if the same measure of Y has been used on both occasions, or from comparison of Y_2 and Y'_2, as in the after-only study.

Evidence about other factors. As in the after-only study, random assign-

[7] In the statistical literature, this kind of matching is referred to as "blocking." For more detailed discussions of the effects of blocking in increasing the sensitivity of an experiment, see Cox (1958a), Feldt (1961), or Lindquist (1953).

[8] Procedures for such analysis may be found in Lindquist (1953), McNemar (1962), and other statistical texts.

ment provides the major assurance that the experimental and control groups did not differ in characteristics that might have led to differences between Y_2 and Y'_2. If the initial measure is of some characteristic other than Y but likely to influence it (for example, if an intelligence test is used as an initial measure in a study where Y represents school performance), comparability on this measure constitutes further evidence that differences in Y are not the result of differences in this relevant characteristic, and thus strengthens the grounds for inferring that the experimental variable, X, was responsible for differences in Y_2.

As in the after-only design, it is assumed that outside events, and maturational or developmental processes, are the same for experimental and control groups. Comparing *change* scores of the two groups provides an estimate of the effects of X after these other influences have been taken into account. Like the after-only study, however, this design does not take account of possible *interaction* between the experimental variable and other events or processes.

The possibility that the research procedures themselves (other than the intentional introduction or manipulation of X) may have influenced Y is greater in a before-after study than in an after-only study. Specifically, the pretest may in itself have an effect. Measures of ability often yield higher scores on a second administration, simply through a practice effect. If the experiment is concerned with attitudes, the initial measure may have still greater effects, by crystallizing the attitudes or exhausting the good will of the subjects. A subject may try to give responses on the second measure that are consistent with previous responses or to make responses "interesting" by varying them from one occasion to the next.

If the effect of the initial measure on subsequent scores is a simple direct one, it will be reflected, along with the influence of outside events and maturational processes, in the difference between before and after scores of the control group and can thus be ruled out as an explanation of differences. However, there is always the possibility of *interaction* between the initial measure and the experimental variable. For example, the experience of being queried in detail about one's attitudes toward race relations or war or capital punishment may draw an individual's attention to these topics. Then after seeing a film that has had one of these themes woven into the plot, the individual may perceive implications stemming from the sensitizing effect of the previous questioning and thus react differently to the film.

An example of a pretest-posttest study. Although there is general agreement among social scientists that behavior is shaped by its consequences, we are still far from understanding the quality of many consequences. The recent surge of interest in behavior modification emphasizes, in part, that reward increases the likelihood of occurrence of the rewarded behavior. Applications of this notion have been manifold in therapy, education, and social engineering. A simple deduction from the general perspective suggests that behavior can be shaped and maintained through provision of extrinsic reward. Token economies are based on this supposition.

Human learning, however, is quite complicated. An issue in the debates over behavior modification has been the extent to which provision of extrinsic reward may lead to behavior that will persist only with continued outside reward and fail to become internalized. One perspective on the situation is provided by self-perception theory, which proposes that people evaluate their own behavior and draw inferences about its meaning (Bem, 1972). Grossly put, people infer they are afraid because they observe their hearts pounding and their hands sweating.

A proposition suggested by this theory is that a person's intrinsic interest in an activity may be *decreased* by inducing that activity as a means to an extrinsic reward. As conceptualized, "overjustified" behavior undermines one's intrinsic reason for doing it. This hypothesis was investigated in a study of preschool children (Lepper, Greene, and Nisbett, 1973). Since the hypothesis specifies a change in behavior, the investigators chose a pretest-posttest design. Drawing with magic markers was the activity selected. Measures of nursery school children's interest in the activity were taken by means of unobtrusive observation at a set location in the nursery school, with the materials available for an hour-long period each day. Three groups were then constituted for the experimental sessions. The first group was asked to draw pictures in order to win an award; the second, to draw pictures with no expectation of award but subsequently given a prize; the third had no expectation of award nor was any given. After about a week, standard observations were again made, with the drawing materials present as before.

In selecting children for the treatments, those who had shown the most interest during the pretest were taken. Random assignment was then made to the three groups. The design permitted an assessment of change following the introduction of the independent variable (anticipated reward, unanticipated reward, and no reward). Although the investigation could have been done with the first two groups, addition of the controls strengthened the design by permitting assessment of what mere attention to the child and the activity would do. Unanticipated reward adds plausibility to the findings by providing the same outcome but in the context of different motivation. It was found that neither the controls nor the unanticipated reward groups changed their behavior from pretest to posttest, while the expected reward group showed a significant decrease in the activity.

Pretest-posttest designs are frequently used in social research, especially when the hypothesis concerns a change in attitude, belief, or behavior as a consequence of some independent variable. The "classic" experiment comprises an experimental and control group, measured before and after. An advantage is the degree of precision introduced by the pretest, since change scores can be examined, or posttest scores adjusted for pretest values. In addition, many hypotheses relate change in some mediating variable as the causal connection between independent and dependent variables: hypotheses concerning the effects of attitudes or emotions on behavior are often of this form. Their testing calls for demonstration of change in the presumed mediating factor.

C. Extended designs

Since the purpose of a design is to operationalize the hypotheses and reduce ambiguity in the interpretation of results, it is easy to see that more complicated arrangements can be worked out for experiments. If, for example, the investigator wants the precision afforded by pretesting but is concerned about reactivity, including the potential for interaction between pretest and treatment, the pretest-posttest *and* posttest-only designs can be combined in one experiment. At least four groups are necessary for this type of design: experimental and control groups with pretest and posttest, plus experimental and control groups with posttest only. This arrangement

Solomon four-group design

is known as the "Solomon four-group" design and is one of a family of extended designs. While used rarely, it has some powerful merit in pinpointing the effects of the factors studied. Schematically, the design is as follows:

Experimental group I: $R \ Y_1 \ X \ Y_2$
Control group I: $R \ Y'_1 \quad \ Y'_2$
Experimental group II: $R \quad \ X \ Y''_2$
Control group II: $R \quad \quad Y''_2$

The first experimental group is measured with respect to Y before it is exposed to the experimental variable; the second is not. Both receive the same experimental treatment. Of the two control groups, one receives an initial measure of Y, at the same time as the initial measurement of the first experimental group; the other does not. All four groups are measured with respect to Y after the two experimental groups have been exposed to the experimental treatment.

This design is especially useful in studies of the effects of early experiences on developmental processes; in fact, Solomon and Lessac (1968) maintained it is the only adequate design for such studies. Using as an example experiments concerned with the effects of isolation or of deprivation of specific stimulus events or behavioral opportunities during early life on the development of various abilities, they argued as follows: A before-after design involves serious problems about possible effects of the initial measure. An after-only design is free of this problem but interpretation of its results is difficult. For example, if on the posttest the control (nonisolated, nondeprived) group scores higher than the experimental (isolated, deprived) group, all one can say is just that. Given such a finding, investigators tend to assume that the reason for the difference is that the experimental group did not develop the relevant abilities because it was not given adequate stimulation or opportunities for learning. However, Solomon and Lessac pointed out that, without an initial measure, there are a number of other possible reasons for the difference. Parallel reasoning applies to "enrichment" studies, in which the experimental group is given a more than ordinarily stimulating environment or set of experiences.

An example of an extended design. A study on risk preferences illustrates the use of such an extended design (Gaskell, Thomas, and Farr, 1973). The "risky shift" effect has been reported and debated for a number of years (Vinokur, 1971): individuals in groups make decisions involving greater risk than their initial preferences and than individuals alone. Much of the research has been based upon one testing instrument, utilizing a set of vignettes about choices faced by persons, with the subject recommending a choice under conditions of greater or lesser risk. Study of risky shift typically employed a pretest-posttest design in which change in choices was assessed. Gaskell, *et al.* (1973) pointed out that the pretest could influence the outcome, either directly, or indirectly through interaction with subsequent treatment or posttest.

In their study, the basic comparisons were of risk decisions made after group discussion and after individual study of the decision items. To assess the effect of pretesting, both a pretested group and a group not pretested were included. Thus, the design involved four groups (individual versus group decisions, pretested versus not pretested). A further elaboration led to inclusion of a fifth group of controls who were tested initially, but not otherwise, in order to assess the effect of anticipating group discussion. The subjects, seventy-five undergraduates, were randomly assigned to the groups.

Although the results were complex, the investigators found that pretesting had an effect in introducing a cautious bias for the individual treatment condition. At the same time, more risky decisions were made after group discussion, even where no pretest was involved. Thus, the investigators found that risk preferences are affected by group discussion over bias introduced by pretesting. Interestingly, the pretest bias affected only those items pretested and did not generalize to other items. In general, the design helped rule out some possible explanations for risky shift.

Taken as a whole, this design made it possible to disentangle the effects of the experimental treatments, the pretest, contemporaneous events, plus interaction between pretest and treatment.

In this type of analysis, it is assumed that if the second experimental and control groups had been tested, their initial scores would have been similar to those of the first experimental and control groups, since all four groups had been constituted by random assignment. Thus, the second experimental and control groups can each be assigned a hypothetical initial score corresponding to the average of the pretest scores of experimental group I and control group I, thus providing a base line for estimating changes in experimental group II and control group II. Since both parts of the experiment are carried out at the same time, it is assumed that all four groups have been exposed to the same contemporaneous events and the same maturational or developmental processes.

Control group II provides a measure of the influence of *maturation* on performance. Change in the performance of experimental group II reflects combined effects of *maturational processes* and the *experimental treatment*. Maturation and experimental effects may not be related, or they may have cumulative effects, or they may run counter to each other, or they may interact in some other way in terms of the way that they affect the dependent variable.

Comparison of the posttest scores of control groups I and II shows the effects, if any, of the *pretest itself* on performance. Change in the performance of experimental group I reflects the *combined effects of pretest and experimental treatment*. The difference between the posttest scores of experimental group I and control group I reflects the effect of the *experimental* variable (and of *maturation or other events*). The difference between the posttest scores of experimental group I and control group I, as compared with the difference between the posttest scores of experimental group II and control group II, reflects *interaction between* the *pretest* and the *experimental treatment*.

As noted above, various comparisons can indicate the effects of the experimental treatment and of maturation combined, for pretested and not pretested subjects, and the interaction of the pretest with the experimental treatment. The effects of the experimental treatment per se can be inferred from comparison of the combined posttest scores of the two experimental groups with the combined posttest scores of the two control groups, assuming no interaction between pretest and treatment. In addition, comparison of the change in performance of experimental group II (that is, the difference between its posttest score and its pretest score) with that of control group II assesses treatment effects, free of any pretest effects.

Other extended designs. Basically, all of the designs considered thus far involve the comparison of an experimental group subjected to a given treatment with an alternative, whether another treatment or no treatment. Some designs provide for disentangling treatment effects from potentially disturbing effects, such as pretests or contemporaneous events. It is possible to extend the designs to comparison of several treatments simultaneously. In fact, the designs can be extended to answer questions about combinations of effects by making them multifactorial. Berkowitz's study of aggression, described earlier, was actually such a design. In addition to comparing two interpretations of filmed events, the investigators utilized two different films—one depicting a prize fight, the other a football game. Four separate groups were used: aggressive interpretation plus prize fight film; aggressive interpretation plus football film; neutral interpretation plus fight film; and, neutral interpretation plus football film.

factorial experiments

Factorial experiments permit analysis of two or more factors simultaneously. They introduce an efficiency that is not possible with single factor experiments and provide information on whether the variables *interact*, that is, produce a combined effect beyond simple additive effects.

An example is an experiment by Marquis (1969), which concerned the effects of two different interviewing techniques on the reporting of chronic conditions in household morbidity surveys. The two techniques were, first, adding descriptive phrases to the usual questions about chronic conditions, and, second, using verbal reinforcements to encourage reports. There were, thus, shorter or longer questions, with or without reinforcements (see table 5.1).

In this 2×2 design, four groups of subjects were used. It should be noted that group B, shorter questions and no reinforcement, represented a control group in that it received the ordinary, or base-line, treatment. The simple effect of reinforcement can be assessed by comparing the columns: groups A and C versus groups B and D. The simple effect of question length can be evaluated by comparing the rows: groups A and B versus groups C and D. In addition, interaction is detected by comparing the diagonals A and D versus B and C, which will indicate that a combination effect is present.

The experiment was done to compare these procedures in eliciting complete and valid data regarding chronic conditions, where the standard was information obtained from the subjects' physicians. Respondents were women aged eighteen to sixty, living in Detroit. Groups of four were matched by geographic area and age, then randomly assigned to the four different treatments. From the various comparisons made, the results indicated that both longer questions and reinforcement improved reporting, but there was also an interaction effect—longer questions improved reporting in the absence of reinforcement but not when reinforcement was used.

Besides the efficiency of the design, it is only through factorial experiments that combination effects can be detected. Such designs, whether pretest and posttest or posttest only, can be extended to more than two factors and to factors at more than two levels. These designs can be analyzed by multivariate methods, the most common being analysis of variance.

TABLE 5.1   Marquis' Four Treatment Conditions[a]

	Reinforcement	*No Reinforcement*
Shorter Question	A	B
Longer Question	C	D

[a] From Marquis (1969).

V. DESIGNS WHEN THE INVESTIGATOR HAS LESS CONTROL

All of the research designs discussed so far in this chapter presuppose that the investigators (or others with whom they are in cooperation) have control both over the independent variables and over the assignment of subjects to conditions and that this control is used to assign subjects randomly. Investigators working in an experimental laboratory have this degree of control, and, within the social sciences, these designs have been used primarily in the experimental laboratory. Nevertheless, their use has not been limited to the laboratory, and, within recent years, there has been an increasing trend toward carrying out controlled experiments in naturally occurring field settings.

One may think of Sherif's summer camps as experimental laboratories, in which the investigator was able to simulate all the features of an "ordinary" summer camp, so that the subjects saw themselves simply as participating in naturally occurring events, although in fact the investigator controlled the crucial conditions. It is conceivable, however, that these studies could have been carried out within one or more already existing camps, provided their directors and staff were willing to carry out the procedures necessary to establish the experimental conditions and to make the necessary observations or to provide opportunities for the investigators to do so in such a way that they appeared to the boys as somehow part of the normal camp personnel.

The Marquis study of the effects of interview techniques on reporting illustrates a "field experiment" in which the investigators had sufficient control so that an after-only design with a control condition could be used. There was random assignment to the treatments, and delivery of the treatments was under the experimenter's control.

Occasionally an investigator may even be fortunate enough to find a real situation with the elements needed for one of these experimental designs, even though the investigator has had no part either in setting up the experimental conditions or in assigning subjects to them. For example, Siegel and Siegel (1957) took advantage of the fact that at their college there were row houses (former sorority houses that the school had taken over) and dormitories, that more students wanted to live in the row houses than there were spaces available, and that a lottery system was used to determine which students would have first choice of living arrangements. From the point of view of investigators, the lottery provided two randomly assigned groups—women who wanted to live in a row house and were able to do so, and women who wanted to live in a row house but were assigned by the lottery to dormitory housing—plus a group not randomly assigned who had chosen to live in dormitories. These investigators studied changes in reference groups and associated changes in attitudes and values. Thus,